Giants *of* Steam

Giants *of* Steam

David Burke

Australia's last

Giants *of* **Steam**

IRON HORSE PRESS

David Burke

Australia's Last

Giants of Steam

Published by the Australian Railway Historical Society
67 Renwick Street Redfern New South Wales 2016

© David Burke. First published 2000

Design Ken Gilroy **Film Separations** KFK Advance Graphics, Sydney **Printed** in Singapore

This book is copyright. Apart from any fair dealing for the purpose of private study, research, criticism or review, as permitted under the Copyright Act, no part may be reproduced by any process without written permission. Inquiries should be addressed to the publisher.

National Library of Australia Cataloguing-in-Publication entry:

Burke, David. 1927 – Australia's Last Giants of Steam

Bibliography.

Includes index.

ISBN 0 909650 47 0

Front Cover photograph: *South Australian 720 class, built at Islington Workshops, standing in Mile End Roundhouse, Adelaide. PDSRM Archives*
Back Cover photograph: *Driving wheels and motion of a New South Wales AD60 Beyer-Garratt. Dale Budd*

Wal Jack / PDSRM Archives

The story of
Australia's goliaths
of the rails
and the men
who made them.

Hauling the Trans-Australian Express, C67
pauses at Zanthus in 1938, the year of its
completion by Walkers Ltd of Maryborough, Qld.

ABBREVIATIONS

ARHS	Australian Railway Historical Society
ASG	Australian Standard Garratt
CME	Chief Mechanical Engineer
CR	Commonwealth Railways
EBR	Emu Bay Railway Company
EMD	Electcro-Motive Division of GM
GM	General Motors Corporation
NSWGR	New South Wales Government Railways
PDSRM	Port Dock Station Railway Museum
PSI	Pounds Per Square Inch (boiler pressure)
QR	Queensland Railways
SAR	South Australian Railways
SRA	State Rail Authority (NSW)
TGR	Tasmanian Government Railways
VR	Victorian Railways
WAGR	Western Australian Government Railways

To my wife Catherine

Pacific type 3830 and 3813 built in NSWGR Workshops, head the famous 'delivery run' of the Spirit of Progress *to Sydney in April 1962.*

ARHS Resource Centre

The Gauges
Broad
        5ft 3in (1600 mm) - H220, 720, 520
Standard
        4ft 8$\frac{1}{2}$in (1435 mm) - C, AD60, C38
Narrow
        3ft 6in (1067 mm) - C19, S, Q, BB18$\frac{1}{4}$

Foreword by Tim Fischer

One of the greatest tragedies of our rail heritage is that the four streamlined broad gauge *Spirit of Progress* locomotives, built to handle Australia's first modern express train between Albury and Melbourne, were all destroyed in the sixties. This is a shocking indictment of those who made the decision to scrap them and to this day leaves in difficulty and in the balance a project to recreate these superb passenger express steam engines of high performance and speed.

Another way to make up for such tragedies is to have comprehensive written coverage of the great steam locomotives of Australia such as *Heavy Harry* of the Victorian system – locomotive H220, and the other broad gauge big power in South Australia. In addition this book brilliantly highlights the various Garratt locomotives including the huge AD60 of New South Wales. The superb streamlined 3801 on the standard gauge was a leader of the Pacific class and remains a paramount performer to this day.

The smaller State systems were not without their extraordinary steam locomotives and to this day the Hotham Valley and the Pichi Richi tourist railways, along with many others, make a positive contribution to the retention of key parts of our rail heritage. It should never be forgotten that the steel wheels of the giant steam locomotives on steel rail have one-seventh of the friction of those somewhat fearsome rubber tyred wheels on bitumen surface. This ratio is why rail will continue to re-energise in the 21st Century as we seek to make up for all the rail track ripped up over the last 100 years.

As we look to the future, the rich past of previous phases of rail development should not be ignored and can in fact be a helping hand. My own personal experience with steam locomotives is not so much on the footplate but standing in middle-distance awe as the steam locomotives tugged huge loads up steep grades around the Riverina and elsewhere.

Uranquinty was an absolute nightmare of a station for steam drivers of the Riverina Daylight Express, especially on a frosty morning bound for Wagga Wagga and Sydney. After coming to a halt to pick up one or two passengers maximum at the then Uranquinty Station platform, the enginemen were faced with an awful grade up to Kapooka and then down into Wagga Wagga, but a grade which produced some superb steam engine action – a vista to behold.

Overseas and by a fluke of timing I once had the privilege of seeing the heroic *Mallard* make its 50th Anniversary run from Doncaster to York, celebrating the all-time steam record of 126 miles per hour in the golden era of steam.

It is not impossible that the world will one day see a limited return of steam locomotives for particular freight rail operations, utilising modern design which greatly reduces energy waste. I am advised that in Europe, research and development work is currently being undertaken on a project of this type.

I have no doubt that this book and other books of its kind, in helping to retain detailed knowledge of the steam engine, will by degrees contribute to the scientific work of a super steam locomotive of the 21st Century. I salute the author David Burke and all those involved who record our great rail heritage.

The Hon. Tim Fischer, MP *

* Tim. Fischer was Federal Leader of the National Party, Minister for Trade and Deputy Prime Minister of Australia, and Member for Farrer – and a strong advocate of rail transportation

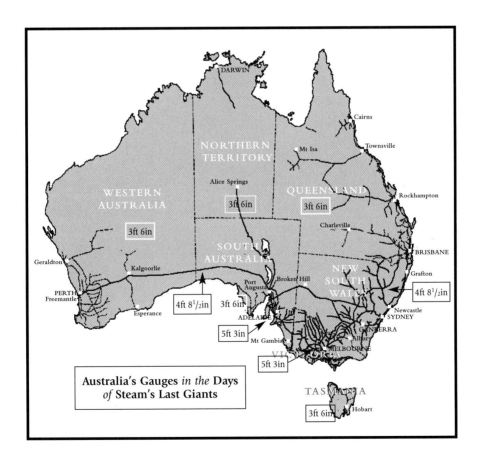

Australia's Gauges *in the* Days *of* Steam's Last Giants

INTRODUCTION

The Last Giants of Steam hail from that other age before Australia fell from grace as a heavy engineering nation; that bygone era when, as with making big ships and other massive machines, Australian workmen proudly built the country's steam locomotives.

Reaching from the 1870s through to 1958 (when the last steam loco was delivered), some 3500 steam locomotives were built in Australian workshops. For close on 70 years many of those same engines were designed by Australian hands. Legions of skilled tradesmen filled government and private company workshops; their tools were the thundering machines that forged the sinews of the iron horse.

The output of Australia's locomotive builders makes an impressive record. No less than 25 plants were regularly engaged at one time or another throughout the country in locomotive manufacturing: Walkers Limited (Qld) 557 engines; Newport–Ballarat–Bendigo (Vic) 534; Clyde Engineering (NSW) 533; Phoenix (Vic) 356; James Martin (SA) 230; Ipswich (Qld) 210; Eveleigh and Cardiff (NSW) 195; Evans, Anderson and Phelan (Qld) 185; Islington (SA) 92; Midland (WA) 65. Some of these machines were copies of overseas imports – mainly from Britain – but at least 20 different classes could be described as 'truly Australian.'

Steps towards independent locomotive design date back to the 1880s when Queensland Railways opened a drawing office in Ipswich Workshops and the first small B15 class appeared. From minor modifications made to locomotives purchased overseas, the techniques and skills gradually came of age.

'Big wheel' design could be fairly said to begin with Victoria's A2 of 1907 and in New South Wales with the NN (C35) of 1914, each a 4-6-0. Gradually other States joined the ranks of railway systems able to produce motive power suited

to the specifications of their own tracks and trains.

Not every result was a 100% success. Major alterations and rebuilds were the price of learning. Some bordered on failure, the wartime Australian Standard Garratt being a prime candidate.

Decorated for State celebrations, C19 no. 702, Centenary, the 100th locomotive completed at Ipswich Workshops in 1923.

QR Historical Centre

From the drawing boards of Eveleigh, Islington and the others, many effective and, in the main, splendid looking locomotives emerged; two Pacifics, the S class of Victoria and the C38 of New South Wales and the 520 4-8-4 of South Australia belong in the gallery of express passenger masterpieces. In freight's less glamorous service, the 720 of South Australia, the D57/58 of New South Wales and Victoria's lone H220 are the embodiment of sheer hulking tractive effort.

But time and the tide of technology wait for no one.

The visit of locomotive engineer Fred Shea to the United States in 1950 to negotiate a license to build the General Motors diesel-electric in a Sydney workshop might be likened to a watershed moment of the Australian railway industry.

Though modified for Australian loading gauge and weight limitations, the GM class diesel of the revitalised Trans-Australian Express and the B class that ousted steam from the *Spirit of Progress* were basically an adaptation of selected American 'off the shelf' prototypes. English Electric diesels delivered to the railways contained the same component of a prime mover, generator, motors and control equipment provided by the original manufacturer, be it in Darlington, La Grange or Schenectady.

The pattern was set. Technology transfer was the name of the game. As many an old timer said - 'things ain't what they used to be.'

None of these remarks is intended to denigrate the achievements of today's engine builders; mostly privately owned (not government!) they produce high horsepower diesels conforming in performance to the world's best practice; observe the 82 class of New South Wales, the NR of National Rail and Queensland's 2800 class.

Irrevocably, progress had to wave farewell to the days when a workshop would take a lump of raw metal and, without needing to go much beyond the gate, hammer out at the other end a gleaming steam goliath. Long departed, too, are the Chief Mechanical Engineers – those all-powerful men with the names of Shea, Young, Ahlston, Pemberton and Mills whose signatures on each drawing testified that this engine was 'all our own work'; fruits of the labours of countless anonymous figures in drawing office, foundry, boiler and machine shop and erecting bay.

The big engines of yesteryear belong to an age when Australia was a gauge-divided nation – broad gauge, standard gauge, narrow gauge, and never the twain shall meet; indeed, even the broad gauge engines of adjoining Victoria and South Australia were forbidden to intrude on the neighbour's tracks. That same broken gauge mentality ruled out any thought of gaining through commonality. That a South Australian 500B could do the work of a D57 or even a H220, or that a Victorian S could double for a 600 or a C36 was apparently a prospect that no self-respecting CME would bother to entertain. By and large, the big engines were creatures of that last stirring era of steam locomotive development, the 1930s when arch tubes and thermic syphons, boosters and mechanical stokers, roller bearings and precision valve gear represented the peak of new technology. Had further improvements not been forestalled by the coming of the diesel, who knows where the path of steam refinement might have taken us?

This book is a pilgrimage into recapturing the majesty and power of steam's last giants. A contemplation of the indefinable quality that set them apart. 'Everything is spherical or cylindrical,' wrote Paul Cezanne back in 1905. The eminent French artist could have been illustrating the eternal shapes that create the fascination of steam locomotion, be it Puffing Billy or a massive Beyer-Garratt. Wheels, boiler, smokebox, cylinders, smokestack, steam domes, headlamp, compressor – all of them speak of nothing if not the cylindrical and spherical, the mystic language of the cosmos.

The intent of these pages is to sniff warm oil mingled with steam, and catch the heady scent of firebox coal as we recall Queensland's chunky C19, the Commonwealth's marathon runner – the C class, the big brute 720 Berkshires of South Australia, Victoria's lone and elegant 'Heavy Harry' and the latter day able narrow gauge Q class of Tasmania and the 'Sammy' of the West. All distinguished in being designed and built in Australia; some are still preserved, memorials to a lost art, the end of the heavyweight line.

The AD60 Beyer-Garratt is the one exception to our local design and workshop rule. Though built overseas, the Chief Mechanical Engineer had the Garratt significantly modified to develop optimum power for New South Wales conditions. As the final and most powerful of all the steam giants it must find a place in these pages. It represents a climax in the development of a world renowned design that was first tried on a slim gauge Tasmanian mining tramway nearly 50 years before.

The wheel spins a full turn. Midland is closed. Newport and Islington are but shadows of past glories. Eveleigh Workshops where they built the C38 is now, in part, a 'high technology park'. The electronics revolution captures the spotlight with devices (and how many of them are Australian?)

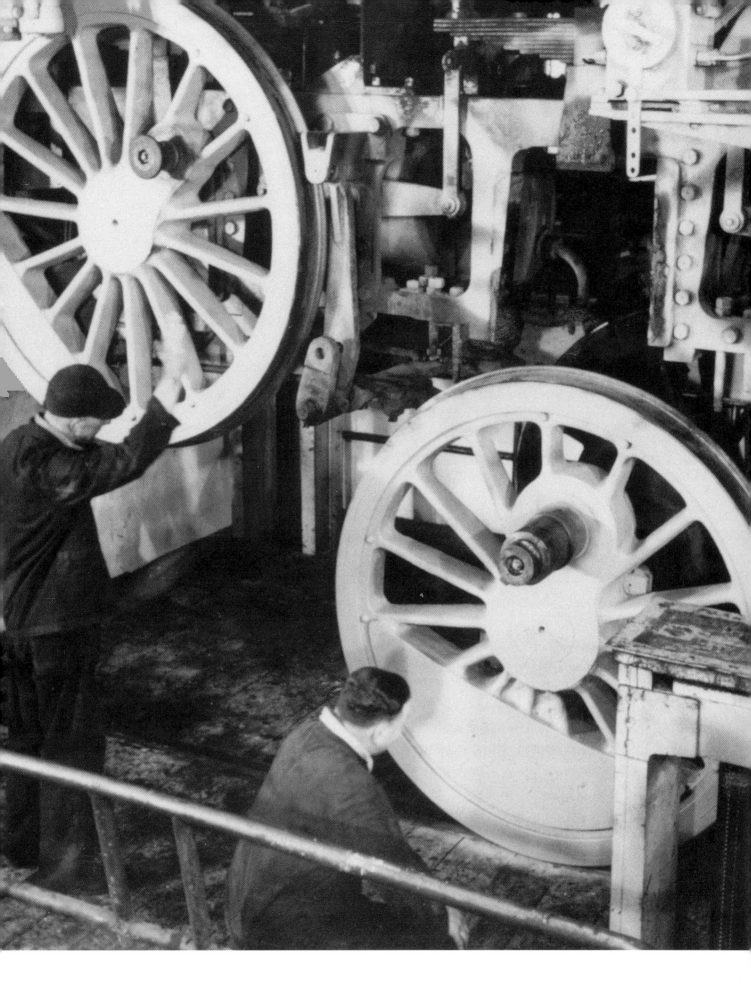

PDSRM Archives

of inconceivable complexity within the space of an infant's toenail. It offers sandwich-slim plastic boxes with glowing screens that at the tap of a key and the blink of an eye connect the owner to limitless catalogues of data stored in some distant country.

Eveleigh's old time locomotive hands had a saying about the parts they forged for the iron horse: 'if you can lift it, then it's not strong enough.' Today's electronics wizards might reply 'if you can see it, then it's too big.'

Far and farewell have we come in a nation that once made steam's 200-tonne locomotives. But consider the echo of a whistle on a frosty night, the blur of speeding siderods, the white plume trailed across green paddocks. Like the artist's painting and the composer's symphony, this is stuff that stirs the imagination and in its spell, the romance of steam's last giants will ever endure.

Working on the driving wheels of a South Australian 520 class at Islington Workshops.

AUTHOR'S NOTE

Locomotives listed as Last Giants of Steam are wholly the a author's preference. Some readers may argue that the selection should have been different – favouring in New South Wales the D57 or 58. The AD60 Beyer Garratt is chosen because it was truly the last of the big line, and in power output it ranked as a giant above the others. But with the Garratt's exception, the qualification for inclusion is that they were locomotives designed and built by Australian railwaymen.

For this reason, the 720 rather than South Australia's larger 500 is the nomination in one chapter. For reasons of chunky size, Queensland's C19 goes ahead of the B18$^1/_4$. And so on. Surviving locomotives in steamworthy condition also include some 'giants' – the QR Beyer Garratt, Victoria's R class and the V of Western Australia are three examples. These machines, and various other steam age survivors, represent the more recent imports from overseas manufacturers; all were purchased in the hectic revitalisation years that followed World War II when Australian workshops found it near impossible to make space for new construction. Some, obviously, are off-the-shelf acquisitions. They are listed in the postscript section on 'Survivors.'

Viewed alongside British and Continental machines, in power rating Australian locomotives compare quite well. But placed alongside the 'giants' of American railroads, the C19 with its 23,000 lb tractive effort and even the AD60 exerting 60,000 lbs pale into respectable insignificance.

The 2-8-8-2 Mallet of the Western Pacific Railroad, exerting a 150,000 lb tractive effort and the 135,000 lbs of the Union Pacific's 4-8-8-4 tell what American 'big power' was all about.

Nor is anything to be gained in comparing the steam age giants with the biggest of the electrics and diesels that supplanted them. The new breed, no matter how spectacularly powerful, belong to a different era of tracks, axle loads and rolling stock operation. Comparison of the past with the present's 4000 horsepower diesels isn't too meaningful. Certainly it is not the thrust of our story, which tells how the largest island continent with a very small population, and far distant from the industrial heart of the Western world, designed and built its own locomotives and sent them steaming into history, playing their unsung role in 'opening up the country.'

Late L. E. Bates / Lloyd Holmes Collection

*Berkshire type
727 in the
Adelaide Hills.*

ACKNOWLEDGEMENTS

To the many friends who generously assisted with information and photographs, the author extends his deep appreciation. Especially recognised are the contributions of Ian Barkla, George Bond, Dale Budd, Andrew Dix, Ron Fluck (Port Dock Station Railway Museum), Tony Gogarty, Adrian Gunzburg, Jim Harvey, Lloyd Holmes, Bill Holmesby, Clive Huggan, David Jones, Peter Kennedy, John Knowles, Brian and Jan Lillis, Catherine Mason, Ian Scutt, Jane Shehadie, Keith Smith, Jim Stokes, David Thurlow, Terry Varney, Jim Wane, Noel Zeplin. Most valued are the writings and correspondence of the late Bill Abbott, John Buckland, Les Haining and Ray Minchin. Thanks to Paddy and Betty for transforming manuscript into computer ready state, and to Srs. Betty and Joy for the generous availability of office equipment. Efforts have been made to ensure all photographs are correctly credited, but where omissions occur, we apologise.

The Last Giants were designed and built in the age of Imperial measurements and, as far as possible, for ease of reading the original specifications are maintained in the text. More detailed data in Imperial and Metric figures is given in the Appendix.

*David Burke
Burradoo, 2000*

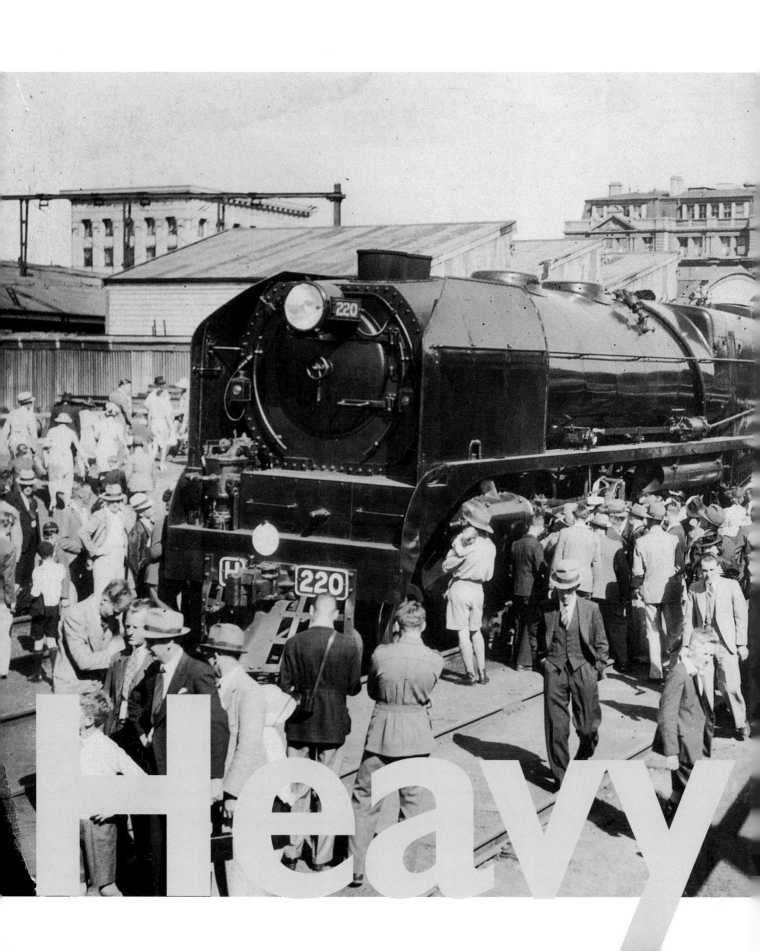

Heavy

CHAPTER 1

VICTORIA's BIG FELLA
THE LONE H220

The story begins with Francis Boardman Clapp, a gold rush migrant from Massachusetts, who became a horse buyer for Cobb and Co's stage coaches. He graduated to a prosperous mail contractor, went on to establish the Melbourne Omnibus Company (a concern that grew to 1600 horses and 178 horse buses) and finally helped launch Melbourne's cable trams. He also gave Australia a railways chief whose name remains a legend.

H220 was barely a week old when 10,000 people came to inspect Australia's then biggest locomotive at Spencer Street Station over the weekend of 15 February, 1941.

Late Guy Bakewell/ARHS Archives

Newport Workshops where more than 500 Victorian Railways locomotives were built between 1893 and 1951. The one and only H220 was the largest of them all.

Harold Winthrop Clapp was born in Melbourne on 7 May 1875. The unenthusiastic student attended Brighton and Melbourne Church of England Grammar Schools and, aged eighteen, secured an engineering apprenticeship at the Austral Otis works, South Melbourne. In 1895 he went north for the electrification of the Brisbane Tramway Company, in which his father was a shareholder. Harold trained horse tram drivers in the mysteries of electric traction, rose to the post of motive power superintendent and drove the city's first electric tram down a South Brisbane street on 21 June 1897.

VR/Author's collection

Railway electrification is the magnet that drew young Clapp to the United States where in 1901 the General Electric Company hired him for the wiring of New York's subways. He transferred to the Pennsylvania Railroad, which was then electrifying lines in West New Jersey and the Seashore district. At Providence, Rhode Island, he and Miss Vivian Noel were wed in 1906 and they settled in New York.

Late J.L. Buckland/Author's collection.

In competitive American society Harold displayed the talent and the qualifications which enabled him to sell himself – just as later he would 'sell' his railways. He went to the sprawling Southern Pacific in California as engineer in charge of extensive commuter electrification projects at Oakland, Alameda and Berkeley. Promotion next took him to the mid-west as vice-president of the East St Louis and Suburban system at the very hub of the nation's transcontinental railroad traffic.

Double-heading the Overland *with veteran A2 class ten-wheelers was intended to be a labour of the past when H220 took up the running.*

In May 1920 Melbourne newspapers announced that Harold was coming home. Whether they realised it or not, the Victorian Railways had bought themselves a keg of dynamite. Harold, tall, lanky, twangy-voiced, caustic of wit, charming, forthright or abrupt as the occasion demanded, was the new Chairman of Commissioners.

The Argus of 16 September reported …

> A tall slim figure in gray tweeds, stepping from the observation car attached to the departmental special that drew up at Spencer Street shortly after noon yesterday, immediately became the centre of interest to a crowd of railway officials. 'I am all for efficiency and teamwork, and want to know my men and my men to know me,' Mr Clapp said in the course of an interview.

VR/Author's collection

'Head Office' in Spencer Street, Melbourne where design of H220 began. Apartment dwellers now occupy the rooms where engineers once planned the 'big fella'.

Harold Clapp was undeniably a character. To trembling stationmasters, apoplectic politicians, white-faced branch heads, outraged wowsers (What, Sunday excursion trains!), he was a man to be reckoned with and never forgotten. He was also a man who got things done. In the 1920s railwaymen dubbed him Clever Mary (a popular detergent of the time) because of his aversion to dust, illustrated by his habit of running a finger along the top shelf during an inspection visit to a stationmaster's residence. He was a natty, fussy person – natty and fussy of his own dress and the same about running a railroad.

During his nineteen years of command from the mighty bluestone edifice on Spencer Street, the Victorian Railways won a reputation as Australia's smartest transport outfit. This was the fruit of Clapp's labours.

Author's collection

Clapp of the Better Farming Trains, Clapp of spreading electrification, Clapp of the cheap weekend excursions, of employing women by the hundreds, of starting a crèche at Flinders Street; Clapp of the superphosphate traffic. Clapp of the Pure Fruit Juice stalls, of the Raisin Bread bakeries, of Travel by Train, Eat More Fruit, On Time All the Time and a host of other slogans.

He was also Clapp of the Newport apprentices' college, of the upgraded crew rest barracks, of painting 'men' (instead of 'gentlemen') on platform lavatories; Clapp, the inspiration of the Australian National Travel Association and the classic Percy Trompf posters that adorned his stations and offices. Said Sir Robert Menzies, once Victoria's Transport Minister and

Harold Clapp's superb Spirit of Progress *with a streamlined S class in charge ready to leave Melbourne on its inaugural journey to Albury on 23 November, 1937.*

Australia's Prime Minister at the time of Clapp's death: 'We have lost a great expert, a great Australian and a great man. He was an outstanding public servant... it is a fortunate country which is able to call to its service men like Harold Clapp.'

Sir Harold Clapp, Chairman of Commissioners, Victorian Railways.

An obituary in the Melbourne *Herald* of 21 October, 1952 reflected on the personality of the dynamic man who had modernised and expanded Victoria's railways...

Restless, brilliant Harold Clapp wove a bright thread in the fabric of Victoria's history. Among the railwaymen of his day he became a legend. He was fussy about the appearance of his rolling stock, and his staff too. As

Veteran T class no. 94 on display with H220 at Spencer Street Station in February, 1941.

Author's collection

Late Guy Bakewell/Author's collection

VR/Author's collection

Gala day at Newport Workshops, 7 February, 1941: Commissioner Chairman Norman Harris addresses the audience at the 'big fella's' launching.

for himself – "His shoes gleamed," a rail veteran said today. "He wouldn't wear shoelaces that were creased – always had spares on hand." He used to fidget at his desk, crossing and uncrossing his legs, jumping up, walking about. (Once a deputation was surprised when he stayed in his chair for two hours; it didn't know he'd just discovered he was wearing odd socks.)

Harold Clapp set high standards; he appreciated good men. But he had a soft spot for the not-so-good. "Heaven knows we make mistakes. But what we try to do is not to have an epidemic of them." Sir Clive McPherson recalls him trudging all the way up the Albury platform to shake hands with the driver of the *Spirit of Progress* to say "thanks for a very good trip".

For the Sydney line Clapp ordered the construction of the swift S class locomotives, a design first considered in 1917 and then shelved.[1] He directed all his engines to be painted a grim, unrelieved black but embraced the Wagner front-end redesign of mainline locos in the cause of better steaming efficiency; he introduced welded rail, electric headlamps, all-steel

A view of the massive siderods and Walschaert valve gear reveals the connecting drive to H220's inside cylinder valve. Germany is believed to have introduced the only other three-cylinder 4-8-4 types.

dining and buffet cars and, in December 1935 with trial equipment imported from America, added to the Sydney Limited [2] historic carriage 36AE – claimed as 'the first air-conditioned coach in the British Empire.' Clapp was ever alert to the growing competition from road and air. During his term he had $1^{1}/_{2}$ hours cut from the Limited's running schedule.

Following his U.S. tour of 1935 he induced a conservative Country Party government to vote him the thousands needed to make his greatest brainchild, the blue and gold *Spirit of Progress* launched in November 1937. After a journey on Clapp's streamliner, smooth, quiet and air-conditioned throughout, who could say that rail travel was on the wane? Who could not say that the broad gauge was in front?

H220's all-steel boiler and the Newport Workshops tradesmen who made it. At 220lbs psi it was in 1941 the highest pressure boiler on an Australian locomotive.

ARHS (Vic Div) Archives

Late Les Poole/ARHS (Vic Div) Archives

But for the depression and then another World War he might have put into operation many more schemes on the railway system forever associated with his name. Which brings us to H220.

Since the early 1930s, Clapp had been planning to improve the Melbourne – Adelaide service with something of the same flair as he intended for interstate trains on the North-East line. On the 131 miles (210-km) between Melbourne and Ararat, particularly on the first section to Ballarat, the *Overland* nightly faced one of the steepest climbs on a VR mainline. Two veteran A2 ten-wheelers were necessary to heave the 10 or more cars, comprising mostly heavy six-wheel bogie wooden stock, up the nine miles (15 km) of the 1-in-48 Ingliston bank to reach Ballarat, and onwards to Serviceton where interchange with South Australian engines took place.

A more powerful locomotive was the obvious key to accelerating the Adelaide service; even eliminating an A2 water stop at Ballan could save 15 minutes. But while Newport's high-wheel S class, barely 10 years old, were ready-made for fast running on upgraded track with 90lb rail to Albury, the Western line relied on engines first produced in 1907.[3]

In November 1935 and again in February 1936 Branch heads met in the Chairman's office to brief him and Traffic Commissioner, Mick Canny on locomotive designs which the Traffic and Rolling Stock branches had devised to run the *Overland*. The selection ranged from a 4-8-2 scheme originated in 1923 which transitioned to a 4-8-4, first conceived on paper in 1929 and latterly upgraded to a larger three-cylinder machine.[4] Harold wanted an engine powerful enough with 550 tons in tow to make mincemeat of the Western grades. This is the engine he told his branch chiefs to go away and build. Not one – but build *three*.

The specification promised a capability for non-stop (ie, non-refueling) running between Melbourne and Ararat, achieving not less than 20 mph (32 kph) on the 1-in-48, equivalent to an output of some 2200hp. Indeed, during a 1940s test on the Western line, the locomotive exerted a

Stubby twin stacks and an elongated single dome accentuate sleek boiler lines in this view taken from Wodonga Coal Stage in 1955 - H220's last year in service.

drawbar horsepower (DHP) of 3300 at 50 mph (80kph). Way and Works were simultaneously told to produce a blueprint for renewal of the Western's 80-lb plant and bridge strengthening, particularly on the Ballarat to Ararat section. Ararat itself was to receive a modern roundhouse, the first of its kind in Victoria, with a turntable capable of holding a big locomotive.

Following the Chairman's directive, Chief Mechanical Engineer Andrew Ahlston instructed his Rolling Stock Engineer, T.D. (Tommy) Doyle and Chief Draftsman A.M. (Alf) Hughes to assemble a

Lloyd Holmes/I.R. Barkla collection

team for the 4-8-4 design. In 1937 the drawings started to reach Edgar Brownbill, who commanded Newport Workshops. Parts began to be ordered. In 1939, under the supervision of Foreman Erector Bill Black, construction commenced.

On the seventh of February, 1941 to the cheers of Newport workers, emerged the VR's first 'Pocono' type – H220.[5] The locomotive was a 'new milestone, not only in Victorian history, but Australian history also,' said Chairman Norman C. Harris. Among the three Commissioners grouped on the dais at Transport Minister Hyland's launching of H220 stood the ever restless Harold Clapp, but no longer as head of the VR. With war clouds gathering over Europe, since July 1939 the Federal Government had appointed him Director-General of the country's nascent aircraft industry, centered upon a couple of Melbourne's windswept paddocks close to the mouth of the river Yarra, at Fisherman's Bend.

VR/Author's collection

An official Newport Works photograph of H220 taken shortly after completion in February, 1941. With a total engine and tender weight of 260 tons, the 'H' was hailed as Australia's largest locomotive, though in tractive effort it was slightly shaded by the D57 of New South Wales and South Australia's 500B.

One popular figure missing from the ceremony was that of Bob Burrell, Engineer-in-Charge of Locomotive Design in the Rolling Stock Branch. Within two months, the career of the man who had 'lived and breathed' H220 for the past four years sadly ended after a sudden illness. The VR Commissioners marked the passing of this life of 50 years, 34 of them spent in the railways, with the words: 'His masterly contribution to the work that led to the appearance in service of Australia's largest locomotive has earned for Mr. Burrell an honoured place in the history of the Department.'

Over a weekend exhibition at Spencer Street Station on the 15 – 16 February, 10,000 people came to inspect H220 which towered above little T94, an 0-6-0 built at the Phoenix Works, Ballarat in 1884. On the Cinesound newsreels and in the daily press, H220 won 'lead story' status as Australia's largest and strongest steam locomotive. If 'H' stood for 'Harold' readers were told that this was 'Heavy Harry' – a name soon adopted by the general public. (Railwaymen invariably referred to the engine just as 'the H' and sometimes 'the big fella'. Likewise rarely was it called a 'Pocono,' an American term for a 4-8-4.) After dynamometer tests between Melbourne and Wodonga, H220 made its first passenger run with the third division of the down Sydney Express on 10 April. With the 11-car, 405-ton train, the H covered the 33 miles on the upgrades to Heathcote Junction in 50 minutes, which was six minutes less than allowed for an S class.

Only in tractive effort did H220 not take national first place. With its smaller driving wheels, the D57 of New South Wales delivered a thousand pounds more. And since Fred Shea had shopped for booster trucks, South Australia's big 500B had jumped to 59,000lbs to trump them all. But no booster was considered for the H.[6] In VR strategy it was an engine big enough, strong enough and fast enough just as Harold Clapp – now more involved with wings, propellers and Beaufort Bombers – had determined five years before.

But Australia's railways can never dodge the limitations of axle load. On the H's axles, the load was $23^1/2$ tons. The axle load thus far permitted on the 80lb plant of the Western line was 18 tons. That 5-ton difference would demand a lot of track and bridge rebuilding! Herein lies one of the recurrent mysteries bedeviling the Last Giants of Steam. Shea's 720 proved too weighty for the SAR's 60lb track. The NSWGR's Mountain class D57 and D58 were strictly limited in mainline operation – in fact a D57 could not venture north of Sydney. In this vein, that doyen of rail historians, the late John Buckland once called the building of H220 'an incredible decision.' Was Bucko maybe right? Maybe so in hindsight.[7]

The H certainly stood high on the ladder of advanced steam technology among Australian railways in 1941. Arguably it could be termed the most perfect locomotive yet designed and built for service on any State rail system. The passenger speed driving wheel diameter measured 5ft 7in, just two inches less than New South Wales' soon-to-follow C38 Pacific. At 220lbs per square inch, the boiler pressure was then the highest in Australia, before the advent of the C38. At 68.5 square feet (6.3 square metres) the grate was the largest – the NSWGR's D57 at 65 square feet was next in size. Total heating surface measured 3980 sq. ft. At 260 tons engine and tender all up, the weight was the heaviest.

All reciprocating parts were fully balanced. All non-driving wheels had roller bearings. The three cylinders were produced in a single casting.

Other features included bar frames, Franklin power reverse, Simplex Improved Type B mechanical stoker, cross-compound air pump, duplex blast pipes, steam dryer, generous valve travel and simplified conjugating valve gear for the forward-positioned inside cylinder which drove the leading driving axle.[8] The Walschaert geared outside cylinders drove the second axle, and in this divided arrangement lay much of the 'magic' of smooth running H220. The all-steel Belpaire boiler was another splendid success. Relatively stubby and fat between tubeplates – sometimes likened to a Beyer-Garratt boiler – it was rarely short of breath (except on inferior coal) to power the three cylinders. At its burning heart lay the welded steel firebox incorporating a combustion chamber and Nicholson thermic syphons; high quality Maitland coal was to be the specified fuel. The original manual shaker grates were later changed for the air-operated Waugh variety, much to the relief of engine crews.

The H also appeared without the traditional builder's plate, Andrew Ahlston was said to oppose them! In another distinguishing feature, like the streamlined S class, it carried the headlight on its smokebox door.[9]

Stubby twin stacks, fed by twin blast pipes and flanked by the essential VR smoke deflectors were features of the H. Subsequent modifications included reduction to a single cab side window and placing the sandbox atop the boiler resulting in an elongated single

H220 leans into a curve with no.105 Fast Goods near Barnawartha.

Lloyd Holmes

profile dome. With the fitting of the Waugh grate and Cyclone spark arresters, brown coal briquette tests were carried out in July 1949. But a North Melbourne Depot report speaks of a jammed stoker and a myriad of sparks pouring from the smokestack. Result unsatisfactory![10] Major overhauls since the commencement of running in 1941 were completed at 269,000 miles in May 1945, the next at 414,000 and the third at 600,000 late in 1951.

In 1955, the H was withdrawn with 821,866 miles (1,322,619 km) on the clock. Repairs estimated at $600,000 were ruled out: the diesel-electric age was upon us. Clyde-GM B class had been hauling the *Overland* since October 1952 and the more powerful S class diesel was soon to arrive. When the visitor walks among the rows of veteran iron horses of another era at North Williamstown Railway Museum, the massive black bulk of H220 still conveys that impression of crouching power – just waiting to be unleashed. Just waiting for someone to load nine tons of coal and 14,000 gallons of water into the hulking six-wheel bogie tender; just waiting for someone to light its fire, power up the stoker and whistle away into the North Eastern night.

'Engine Requirements' at Seymour; the blanked cab second window is evident.

Lloyd Holmes/I.R. Barkla collection

In May 1992, the then Premier, Mrs Joan Kirner visited the Museum for the unveiling of a plaque in honour of all the sung and unsung who had designed, built, crewed and maintained H220. Should we be too critical of the powers-that-be of sixty years ago for the decision to build a locomotive so mighty as H220? World War 2 intervened. Harold Clapp was no longer in charge. Upgrading the Western line was shelved; post war it was more important to get the VR back on its feet, to face the challenge of those 'other forms of transport.'

Thus H220 remained the one and only 'Pocono' to emerge from Newport. The bar frames and boiler plates destined for numbers 221 and 222 gathered dust in the Erecting Shop for almost twenty years before going to the scrapyard. Ararat won its impressive new roundhouse – a sort of rival for Junee in New South Wales – with an 85ft table large enough to turn the

H (which measured 92½ft overall). Yet except for a carefully monitored trial with a Dynamometer car and 680-ton freight on 5 and 6 May, 1949 Ararat never sheltered the 'big fella' and the table never wore out turning it.[11] Once more, fate by miscalculation had visited a Last Giant of Steam.

However evidence from as far back as May 1946 suggests the VR may have harboured second thoughts about running H220 and its yet unbuilt mates on the Western line. In that month, two

Hand on the Westinghouse brake valve, watchful eye on the gauge, Driver Bert Baker Snr. makes a continuity brake tests on H220 while waiting to leave Seymour with the 'Up' fast goods in 1953.

Lloyd Holmes/I.R. Barkla collection

senior Rolling Stock engineers, W D Galletly and W H Chapman visited Beyer, Peacock's office in London to discuss the design of a 'double Pacific' Garratt which would run at express speed on 80lb rail while retaining the A2's axle load of 17¼ tons; tractive effort would be equal to H220.[12] With the *Overland* beyond its reach, the H had been switched to priority wartime traffic, rostered for the express freight service that kept supplies moving on the interstate rails. The North-East line, upgraded by Clapp for *Spirit of Progress* performance became H220's territory for the rest of its working life.

Nightly at 9.25 it would whistle away from Melbourne Yard with No. 105 Fast Goods and a load of 820 tons bound for the border. A North Melbourne crew took it to Benalla; Benalla men went through to Wodonga and after resting returned home next morning, leaving Wodonga Coal Siding at 8.45am with No. 44 Fast Goods to Melbourne. Freight speeds, depending on rolling stock, went from 45 mph (72kph) to 50 and 55 mph (80 and 88kph). Five round trips totalling around 1900 miles (3040km) were made week-in, week-out.

H220 did achieve isolated moments of glory hauling the *Spirit* much as 5719 had been tried from Sydney on the Melbourne Limited in 1941. The occasions were in February 1944 and again in July 1947 – each time taking the 550-ton train from Spencer Street in the evening and returning on the 'Up' next morning.[13] Permitted speed was 60 mph (96 kph), arrivals were right on time and, as is the habit of big engines, 'it went uphill as fast as it came down.'

The men who crewed and maintained the H seldom had a hard word to say about the 'big fella' except for the coal dust that rained down on the cab from the twin stacks, or when a lower grade coal had to be substituted for the prime Maitland fuel which the locomotive was optimally designed to burn. Placing a dampened hessian sack over the footplate screw conveyor hatch was one trick used by the crew in trying to lessen the dust.[14]

A North Loco fitter commented: 'A mate of mine at Seymour Depot built a house on his overtime from the S class. But the H wouldn't give you enough overtime to start on a backyard dunnie.'

According to the late Les Haining, a senior driver-instructor who spent years on H220...

The H was a mighty engine with an outstanding free-steaming boiler. Yes, a wonderful steam generator. It went like a dream on Maitland coal, which was usually reserved for it. It was another story when they had to switch to Lithgow or State Mine – the firebox filled with ash, or that imported Indian muck that ran through the grate like treacle. Then we'd be losing time at Seymour or Benalla, bailed up over the pit cleaning the stuff out.

Another problem for the crew is when smoke rolled back on the cab, which it would do under certain conditions. It made things pretty dirty. That's why we used goggles on the H. Otherwise it was the best all-round loco the VR ever built. The best loco I ever ran.[15]

Author's photograph

Enginemen commented on the smooth riding of H220, and the regular 'huffada-da-puffada' beat from the twin stacks, rarely out of 'sync.' The divided drive from the three cylinders was less damaging to the track. The inside valve derived its motion from a rotating 'bell crank' shaft located beneath the boiler, rather than from Gresley style levers above the forward buffer beam which tended to be subject to frame stress and resultant inaccuracy. A three-cylinder 4-8-4 was a rare machine and VR engineers took their design cue from the German builder, Henschel and Sohn who applied the 'rotating' gear to Prussian State Railways' G12 series 2-10-0, and also to locomotives for Spain and South America.

As a young fireman, Jim Seletto recalled being rostered on an old D3 (4-6-0) assigned to double-head with H220 and, because of coupling strength, was placed in front of the H ...

Cold and silent, yet thankfully saved from the scrap merchants, H220 since 1962 has been in the care of the Australian Railway Historical Society (Victorian Division) at the North Williamstown Railway Museum.

We moved to the mainline at Kensington, and the exhaust from the H220 began to grow stronger. Looking back, all we could see was this huge smokebox towering above the D3's tiny tender.

Speed increased, as did the H's exhaust beat. By the time we had reached the bottom of Glenroy Bank (2 miles of 1-in-50 on the Broadmeadows line), the speed was up to 30mph. Then the incredible roar of the H's exhaust started close-up. From that moment the frightened little D3 merely skimmed the rails, doing its best to keep from being trampled by the roaring black monster behind. At 30mph we hurtled up Glenroy Bank, speed rose to 45 mph frequently beyond Broadmeadows as the other crew put the H to the test.

We flew up Beveridge, and again over the Divide at Heathcote Junction which we topped at 30mph and rolling. I'll never forget the terror I felt when H220 opened up in the attack on Glenroy Bank, or that roaring exhaust. 'Hell!' I thought, 'what if we derail or hit a cow, or have a level crossing smash – the H will run straight over us, and not even notice!'[16]

Lloyd Holmes, now retired to the North Coast had the distinction of working for both the VR and NSWGR. So, hopefully, he can't be accused of a one-eyed opinion when he recalls his first sight of H220 as it steamed from Wodonga sidings – 'I took in the powerful, handsome features of what was then Australia's largest steam locomotive and made the inevitable comparison with the D57 class of my home State. Whereas the latter were rough-hewn and angular beasts of burden, never meant to grace the front of a passenger train, H220 was a comparatively refined monster whose overall lines had been subject to much aesthetic consideration, befitting a locomotive intended for passenger service.'[17]

His career as a Train Examiner allows him to relive the memory of H220 passing in the night...

The cadence of its inimitable three-cylinder beat, powerful headlight probing the track ahead, smoke from the twin funnels trailing back highlighted by the shaft of fire-glow spearing out from the parted fire-doors; a glimpse of engrossed figures in the rosy-hued cab; spinning driving wheels, flashing rods, and Walschaerts gear illuminated by the lights mounted beneath the running board. And all too soon it was past, the noise diminished, replaced by the clicketty-clack of dark, bobbing wagons, until three red tail lamps defined that Number 105 was on its way.

Another occasion relates to a remarkable run of 10 February, 1944 when, due to an S class shortage, H220 was assigned to the Down *Spirit* from Spencer Street to Albury. Driver Alex Reid and Fireman Lynch of Wodonga Depot, were on the rather crowded footplate. Riding with them were Assistant C.M.E. Edgar Brownbill and Superintendent of Loco. Maintenance George Brown.[18] Alex Reid breasted Oliver's Bank (as the Glenroy grade was also known) – a long and heavy pull, often bringing the S Class back to 12mph – at 45 mph, with 190lbs steam pressure on H220's gauge. At Heathcote Junction, 33 miles out and the summit of the long climb from Melbourne, they were 16^1/$_2$ minutes up on the timetable, 7 mins ahead at Seymour. Near Euroa, Alex throttled back the H and had the *Spirit* 4^1/$_2$ early at Benalla then easily kept 4 to 5 mins ahead of schedule until the Murray River bridge where a 10 mph 'Perway' slack applied, bringing them two minutes early into Albury platform. Alex recalled Mr Brownbill's face black with dust generated by H220's stoker and looking 'more like a Kentucky Minstrel than the Assistant Chief Mechanical Engineer!'[19]

Les Haining whose father was an Acting Leading Hand on H220 boiler construction, finally recalled a humorous moment related to the H's ability to reel off the miles at top speed...

Let me finish with a true story. Prior to leaving Benalla at 12 noon on the Up, the guard – quite a comic from Seymour – said I want to back a horse in the Seymour races at 1.40pm. OK, Tom, tie yourself in. Away we went, pulling up in Seymour Yard at 1.30pm. Not bad, I thought, 60 miles in 1^1/$_2$ hours, allowing H220 was then limited to 45 mph with four-wheel stock. Anyway, we were waiting for the guard – very thankful I expected him to be. But he said, "You're a bloody maniac, Les. You cut 20 minutes off the timetable. I missed the meal allowance and my horse got beat!"[20]

Yes, to the men who crewed and maintained the 'big fella', this Last Giant of Steam was a mighty machine.

To the bark of its three-cylinder exhaust, H220 climbs the 1-in-50 grade of the Tallarook bank.

Lloyd Holmes

Though seen many times, the VR Publicity Office's retouched photograph depicting H220 at night on a North East fast freight remains one of the classic images of Australian railroading.

HEAVY HARRY

O Harry you beaut I've heard you roar:
Up the slopes of the great Divide,
And roll away like thunder down
The grade on the other side.

Now he frets all day in the Loco Shed,
And his huge steel frame seems dead;
No steam sings from his whistle stack,
No smoke flies overhead.

They say he's old and broken down,
And nobody knows his fate;
But his heart's out there on the open track,
The lord of the Albury freight.

His great wheels coupled with a cast of power,
To his two-ton piston rods;
And his long lean flow of beauty,
O shades of the Grecian gods.

He longs to speed with the wind again,
Like a Titan that's burst his bars,
To stab the night with his shaft of light,
To fling his steam to the stars.

Then out and away to the great North-East,
Where the straights and the grades are kind,
He mows the miles like a bat from hell
With a load and a half behind.

O there's many an engine haunts the shed,
Who's drivers are long since dead;
But their ghosts come out on the midnight tracks,
When the green light calls ahead.

Then through the cuttings and round the bends,
Their wheels begin to spin,
As they pull their phantom loads again,
And the ghosts on footplates grin.

Their stacks are wet with the flying steam,
As they race down the trail of years;
But the dew is moist as the salted wet,
The wet of the salted tears.

So au-revoir you shadowy crews,
That drove our lords of the line;
We dips our lids to you tonight,
For the sake of auld lang syne.

And I hope that when the powers meet,
Their minds will take a look,
At Harry half hid in smoke and steam,
On the straight to Tallarook.

by J.M. Dunn, A.S.M. Cathkin, originally
appearing in V.R. *Newsletter* May 1958.

H220 is now located at the Railway Museum, North
Williamstown, where it was transferred in April, 1962.

H220 plaque at
North Williamstown
Museum.

Author's collection

VR/Author's collection

South Australia's 'big power' stands side by side
at Mile End in 1935. On the right is no. 502,
built in England by Armstrong Whitworth to an
Australian but strongly U.S.-influenced design
To the left is a very new American-style Berkshire
no. 723, Australian designed and a product of
Isligton Workshops.

Berk

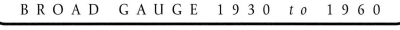

CHAPTER 2

FRED SHEA'S 'BIG MIKADO' THE S.A. 720 CLASS

Fred Shea joined the Victorian Railways as a 16-year-old apprentice at Newport Workshops in 1907. From a humble beginning on 1/9*d* a day, he rose from fitter and turner to become one of the famous Chief Mechanical Engineers of Australian railways in the latter days of steam.

His remarkable career spanned all three ages of the locomotive: from steam to electric, then to the all-conquering diesel. He was a man of guts; resourceful, energetic, an engineer's engineer, an outstanding manager and achiever.

PDSRM Archives

Luck is often a good leg-up on the ladder of promotion, and Fred Shea's good luck, backed by ability, was that his career paralleled the Commissionership of another great railwayman, Harold Clapp. At Clapp's recommendation he joined the South Australian Railways as Chief Mechanical Engineer at a time of enormous change on the broad gauge across the border.

From Newport workshops, his path had led to the drawing office where he assisted in the design of the express Walschaert A2, and later was responsible for introducing the VR's first electric loco, the 1100. Clapp brought him to the attention of William A Webb, the American railroader who in 1922 had crossed the ocean to begin a new life as Chief Commissioner of the South Australian Railways.

At the age of thirty-two Fred went to Adelaide where, like his 'big Yank' boss he found a railway weak of track, archaic of engine and in workshops

William A. Webb, the American railroader appointed Chief Commissioner of the SAR – 1922-30.

Author's collection

Author's collection

A shipment of the new Armstrong Whitworth locomotives fills the deck of MV Beldis at Port Adelaide in 1926.

antediluvian. As a member of Webb's team he would figure in an immense locomotive adventure that changed the face of the SAR and left a mark on Australian railway history.

Leaving the railways, Fred ventured into a world apart; at the outset of World War 2 he joined Clapp in establishing the Government Aircraft Factory. He occupies the unique niche of the locomotive men who in Australia's defence also built bombers.

Teamed again with Clapp post-war, he helped to author the ambitious plan to standardise the nation's rail gauges. While with the Transport Department, he blossomed as writer and broadcaster in defence of the railway against 'other forms of transport' and assumed the role of apologist for the iron horse. He argued that aircraft had a limited role to play, though in his old age he witnessed mass transportation shifting to the skies.

After forty years of government service, and knowing the secure umbrella of the departmental system, Fred Shea went out into the cold. He joined a particularly tough private industry and made a success of it, ushering in the American diesel-electric age while watching steam go to the torch by the rusting hundreds, the price to pay for progress and saving rail from those 'other forms of transport.'[1]

Fred had an innate ability to rise to the challenge, to make things work, whether they be a 720 class or a twin-engined Beaufort. He sought no fame for himself and his life led to no fortune. By lovers of the locomotive he is best remembered for those South Australian days; a grimy faced figure riding the footplate of a 500 class on trial runs, fussing around axle box and bearings to remedy early failures, dirtying his hands in roundhouse repairs, briefing his staff on the sweeping plan he devised for the rebuilding of Islington Workshops – a matter of immense satisfaction in a busy life.[1]

Adelaide's conservatives were due for a shock when Webb settled in their midst and launched his plan to sweep away the outdated operating practices and obsolete motive power of a hidebound railway. In making these revolutionary changes Fred Shea, now 35 years old, was his right-hand man at the introduction of the massive Mountain type 500 class, the tall-wheeled 600 class Pacific, and the medium range 700 class Mikado.

The new era began in March, 1926, when the heavy lift ship, MV Beldis docked in Port Adelaide revealing a deck crammed with engines that looked entirely 'Yankee' but which, for reasons of Empire preference, had been built in England at the works of Sir W G Armstrong Whitworth, of Newcastle-on-Tyne.

The *Railway Engineer* and other international journals were impressed by the ample boiler-to-cylinder relationship (steam generation to steam usage), the generous dimensions of the piston valves and the lengthy (28 in) cylinder stroke common to all three classes. *The Locomotive*, the technical bible of the steam age, published 500 and 600 class drawings 'prepared by the Chief Mechanical Engineer Mr. F.J.Shea, and now building in this country'. The article continued...

> Apart from the engines exported from America for the Peking-Suiyan Railway of China, and some built for Mexico, we believe these will be the largest engines ever built in any country for export. The price of the ten Mountain type is given as £17,590 per engine. These engines are to be used for hauling the Melbourne Express to Serviceton (sic), and are expected to take ten or eleven cars. From the European standpoint, it seems remarkable that these enormous locomotives are to operate on flat-bottomed rails, although we do not yet know what the axle loads are. Of course, in the United States and Canada they regularly use very heavy engines on this style of road. The new engines will be provided with tenders carrying 12 tons of coal and 8300 gallons of water. They are to be fitted with electric headlights and automatic centre couplers.

Shea unrolled his design papers and, settled in digs at Newcastle-on-Tyne, spent weeks hammering out final construction details with the Armstrong Whitworth works management. To oversee the actual construction phase, he had Jimmy Hunter come from Adelaide to take up temporary residence as the SAR's on-site engineer. Shea and Hunter were the two men most intimately involved in the preparation of the original general specifications; between them they shared the common knowledge and objectives of the sort of engines that Commissioner Webb wanted. After Fred's return home, a stream of letters between the two urged Hunter to ensure that the Scotswood plant observed the fine details of the contract, kept to schedule and held to price – all of which made Jimmy a fairly prickly individual to deal with from the manufacturer's viewpoint.

Correspondence between the two men from October 1924 to September 1926 amounted to seventy-six letters and progress reports from Hunter to Shea and sixty-two letters from Shea to Hunter, plus sixty-two cables exchanged from one to the other. While most of the material was on formal technical matters, Fred at times made it abruptly clear that he wanted to hear of no argument for relaxation in the locomotive specifications. Mostly he appears satisfied with the role of his inspecting engineer, but after the first shipment reached Adelaide some of the workmanship did not please him. One cable to Hunter, who was still at the

Scotswood works, asks: 'Conduit fittings for electric light very poor. Why were locomotives not fitted up with the various inspection fittings and junction boxes recommended by the Pyle National? This Company advises me the fittings were supplied to Armstrong Whitworth. Please investigate.'

Double-heading the Melbourne Express with Rx class 4-6-0s – a regular practice before the big engines arrived.

The Scotswood drawing office staff included a 23-year-old leading draftsman who himself was later to leave his *Mountain type no. 500,* stamp on another *the heaviest and most* Australian railway. Fred *powerful locomotive that* J. Mills had been with *Adelaide has ever seen, is* Armstrong Whitworth

an object of deep interest after assembly and test at Islington in 1926. Chief Commissioner Webb is the second figure from the left at the front of the engine.

since 1920 and it is quite likely that he participated in the South Australian project. In 1926 he migrated to the Western Australian Government Railways as a locomotive designing draftsman and advanced to the post of Chief Mechanical Engineer in 1940 (see Chapter 7). During World War 11 he would be responsible for the design of the Australian Standard Garratt (ASG) which had a checkered operating record on State narrow gauge systems. Ironically, as one of his many tasks as a 'fixer', Fred Shea would be recruited to advise on the correction of the ASG's mechanical shortcomings.

The months that followed the arrival of the 500, 600 and 700 classes were among the busiest of Shea's career. At Islington an enlarged doorway had been made in the side of the old erecting shop to provide passage for the new motive power. Each locomotive had to be reassembled, boiler and cab mounted on frame, all the steam and air piping and other controls reconnected. An expert team of tradesmen was assigned to bring each one of the new machines into working order as quickly as possible for trial running. The CME's office issued an exhaustive test procedure before the first member of each class could be made operational. No locomotives of such size and power had traversed the broad gauge before; more so, they contained a great deal of equipment that was completely new to the workshops, crews and running sheds.

Fred took a delight in showing fellow railwaymen over the new locomotives and describing the many advanced features incorporated in the design. He would point to the cast steel bar frames, to each half set of cylinders and smokebox saddle produced as another steel casting, then bolted together; to the compensated springing and such other 'Yank' innovations as the spacious windowed cabs, self-cleaning smokeboxes, M.C.B. automatic couplers, Franklin grease lubricators for the axle box guides. All three classes were designed for easy conversion to standard gauge: wheel centres were 'dished' to simplify a narrowing of the width, while brake hangers were cast with two separate fittings, the second for relocation of the rigging to meet standard gauge specifications. The trailing wheels beneath the wide firebox ensured that no alteration would be required to boiler or frame configuration. The cavernous fireboxes incorporated arch tubes to maximise heating surface – while those with a discerning eye might have noted that the common 'telescopic' shape of the boilers indicated a significant design change from the early sketches of a humped or wagon top boiler which had appeared in the newspaper and

PDSRM Archives

Cab of the 720 class with the mechanical stoker-feed prominent beneath the 'Butterfly' firebox doors. The grate, with an area of 59.58sq ft was designed to cope with poor steaming quality Leigh Creek coal. Later it was reduced to 46.8 sq ft to enhance combustion as the SAR was forced into the era of oil and oil-coal firing.

magazines. Maximum use was made of parts commonality, an area where Fred proved to be a leader in Australian railway practice.

The CME was on the footplate when no. 700, the first locomotive in steam, left Islington on 27 April 1926. As observers watched the impressive Mikado ease its way by veteran Q, S and Rx classes awaiting repair, the full impact of the Webb era became quickly apparent. What an increase in bulk and sheer gargantuan strength! In starting tractive effort the 500 class (as

SAR/Author's Collection

First engine of the Webb era built at Islington Workshops in 1928-29 was the 710 class Mikado. With boosters removed they took over light line duties from the 720 when the Berkshires proved too weighty for branch tracks.

introduced) stood at 192 per cent more powerful than the Rx it was to replace, the 600 rated at 85 per cent higher and nearly three times above that of the high-wheeled 4-4-0 S class it would also supplant. Axle loads soared from a previous limit of approximately 18 tons for the mainlines and 12 tons on branches. Each axle of a 700 carried a weight of some 17 tons, for the 500 it was around 22 tons while the 600 topped the scale with an axle load of some 23 tons. Soon to be dramatically eclipsed were the old Express loads on the Adelaide Hills – around 255 tons with two Rx in front and some 355 tons with a third Rx employed as push-up.

The list of new equipment which had to be mastered by engine crews read like a buyer's catalogue to the best and latest of British and American locomotive practice – air-operated precision reverse gear, power-operated firedoors and ashpan hopper doors, Pyle National turbo-generators for the headlights and cab lights, independent and separate engine automatic air brakes. In the case of the 500, a Duplex mechanical stoker supplied by the Locomotive Stoker Company of Pittsburgh and New York saved the fireman's sweat and tears.

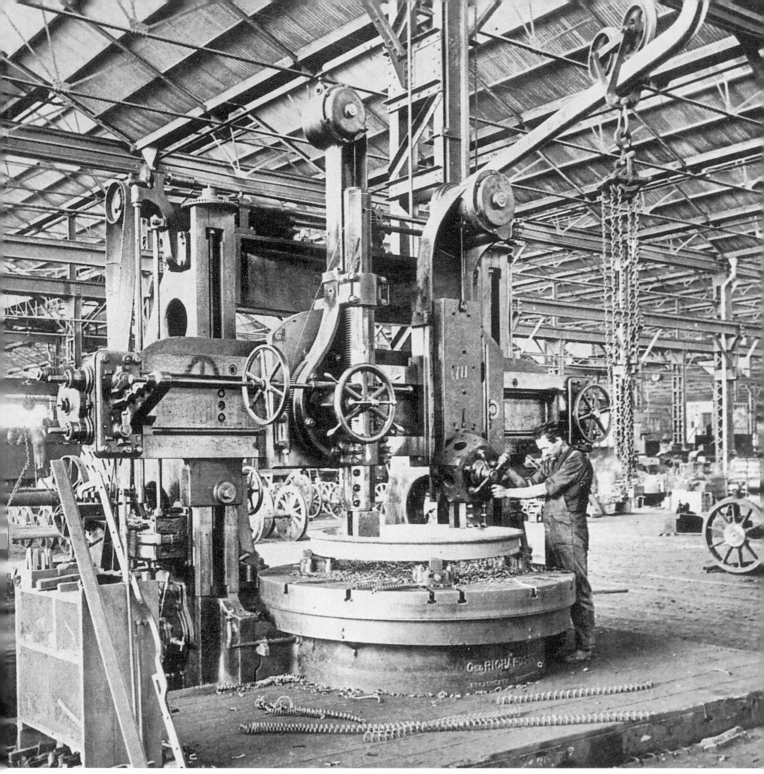

SAR/Author's Collection

Under Fred Shea's direction, the SAR's Islington Workshops underwent a total renewal and by 1928 were regarded as the most modern in Australia.

But in November 1926, a meeting of the Locomen's Federal Executive resolved that hand-firing the 600 and 700 classes imposed too heavy a strain and was 'inconsistent with Australian ideas of what was a fair amount of work for human beings to do.' Clearly it was a dig at the 'Yankee approach' of Commissioner Webb. Further, a Union representative submitted that something like a dozen enginemen had collapsed owing to the tight fit of the big engines in the Mount Lofty tunnels. Drivers were suffering blistered arms while holding the regulator and firemen had to wear gloves while wielding the shovel to save their hands and arms from being seared. Under summer conditions, the Union believed that feeding the big power fireboxes would reach beyond one man's physical endurance. They asked for mechanical stokers on the 700 and especially the 600 and, in the interim, the immediate rostering of two firemen to each engine. Webb would not agree, no doubt recalling engines just as big in America which carried but a single fireman. However he agreed to compromise on the train loads set for the South Line grades, while for traversing the Mount Lofty tunnels, enginemen would be issued respirator hoods – canvas head coverings with eye slit mica spectacles and an air bottle hose connection. One would not have been surprised to hear reports that Men from Mars were abroad in the Adelaide Hills.

Fred Shea, Chief Mechanical Engineer of the South Australian Railways.

Fred Shea was born without the taste of a silver spoon. When he wished, he could easily become 'one of the blokes.' He understood the heat and clamour of the footplate, and in this context was surely not unmindful of the stress and challenge that the American-style big power had suddenly imposed upon enginemen. As with the 500, he also planned to equip the 600 with a mechanical stoker, a conveyor screw trough in the tender floor testifying to this purpose. However for a variety of reasons, mechanically firing the Pacific was not to occur, in one form or another, for quite some time. Thus it was that a fireman on the 600, with maybe more than 500 tons in tow, would be faced with feeding his heavy scoopfuls of coal into a firebox measuring 55 square feet in area. Well may he have sighed for an elderly Rx with its grate of 20 square feet! To compound the fireman's problem, the base of the tender bunker lay some twenty inches beneath the level of the firedoor, demanding a 'lift' as well as a 'lunge' to hurl coal from a loaded scoop into the roaring flames. These were footplate conditions not to be relished on a roasting midsummer day.

The leap from old style engine management to an era of big power technology called for a considerable reapplication of footplate skills. Directed by Loco Superintendent David Collier, driving and firing practice

Author's collection

Right: The 720 was the largest locomotive class built at Islington. Between 1930 and 1943 the workshops delivered 17 big Berkshires on the broad gauge rails.

Below right: Class leader no. 720 pauses at Callington with a Tailem Bend passenger train in April, 1938.

seemingly almost overnight had to shake itself free of the cobwebs of the Rx era. The new locomotives presented drivers with an enormous bulk to manage; a vast boiler profile to see across; and components requiring monitoring and manipulation that represented a real 'state of the art' in modern engine technology. The late Stan Watson, Traffic Manager who worked alongside Fred Shea recalled...

PDSRM Archives

Late J.L. Buckland/Author's collection

> The reaction of enginemen was generally good and co-operative. There was no refusal on the part of any driver or fireman to do his rostered duty. Many were keenly eager to become the first of those required. This attitude applied particularly to first test runs. Drivers certainly took pride in the new monsters and that pride increased as time went by – especially when, early in their introduction, South Australia's new locomotives became a major attraction for tourists.

Old hands of Islington remembered the two smoke-o whistles, one mid-morning, the other in the afternoon when men were allowed fifteen minutes for a cigarette – provided they kept on working. They also recalled the once daily eight minutes allowed for a visit to the lavatory. En route they had to hang up their job tokens at the Timekeeper's office and if the eight minutes were exceeded, or the visit repeated beyond once a day, a 'please explain' might well ensue. Regulations belonging to the 1880s were not easily changed, but for the rest of it, under Mr Webb's command, a workshops metamorphosis was at hand.

Rebuilding Islington was Fred Shea's great achievement. All the desires he once held for Newport Workshops in his VR days were here made possible, not in piecemeal fashion, but in one grand shopping spree financed by an £800 000 allocation from Webb's renewal budget. Now the SAR could claim, as Fred frequently did, to possess the most modern and capable workshops in the nation. No longer did they have a need to import locomotives or other rolling stock. Across Australia, a new dawn of the steam age had commenced. Islington, like Eveleigh, Newport and Ipswich would hold the ability to launch engine power completely designed and built by Australian hands.

By 1928 the workshops had been totally rebuilt: points, crossings and sidings rearranged, 1040 new machines installed, plant equipment linked to individual electric motors rather than driven from a common steam-powered belt (the motors represented a total output of 6500 hp). The Bellis Morcom air compressor was capable of supplying 550 cu metres of air per minute, while the new boring machine could turn out eighteen tyres a day as against a previous rate of four; the tall and powerful gap riveter was equal to handling the most intricate boiler manufacture. For locomotive production, a huge saw-toothed new steel and iron framed building housed the machine, erecting, boiler and smithy's shops. Served by twenty-two overhead cranes, it embraced the entire process of locomotive construction, utilising the American approach to the 'flow through' of materials.

Islington's building of the new 710 class realised a particular Shea ambition. Commissioner Webb arranged a vice-regal party at the workshops on 20 October 1928, the day of the first engine's delivery, the Saturday afternoon event allowing many of the staff to attend with their families. The State Governor, Sir Alexander Hore-Ruthven performed the unveiling of no. 710, which also bore his name. The Governor then 'drove' 710 a short distance down the workshops yard and congratulated Fred and his men on turning out such a fine machine – South Australian designed and built. In effect, the new Mikado was an improved version of the Armstrong Whitworth 700 class, having the same wheels, cylinders and motion of the original imports, while the Islington alterations contributed a larger boiler heating surface, cross compound air pump and a booster located in the Delta cast steel trailing truck; total tractive effort (at 85 per cent boiler pressure) measured 48 000 lbs. Completion of 710 was a matter of immense pride, not only the first fruits of a reborn Islington, but also signalling a fresh epoch in the State's manufacturing abilities. A contemporary SAR booklet, no doubt under Fred Shea's inspiration, hailed no. 710 as 'the most powerful locomotive yet built in Australia.' It hauled, without booster assistance, 'a mile-long train comprised of bogie gondola wagons' between Dry Creek and Gawler. This load embodied what Webb's big power railroading was all about, and better was yet to come.

But another four years of the American 'new broom' proved enough for certain political and union foes. With his contract not renewed, Webb in 1930 departed none-too-happily the South Australian scene. Before farewelling Adelaide, the Commissioner wrote his CME a quite emotional letter in which he said…

During my career as a railway official it has been my good fortune to be associated with several very capable mechanical men: men of outstanding ability, but in reviewing the work which you *A South line freight departing* have done here with me, I do not know of any one of *Mount Lofty; for this 720 most* these men who could have, on their own responsibility, *of the heavy work is over.*

Lloyd Holmes

Sheer brute power seems to exude from the first Berkshire, no. 720 with its American-style centre headlight, lofty cab and in between,

massive boiler. The Works photograph dates from the entry of no. 720 into traffic on 26 November, 1930.   SAR/Author's collection

duplicated the accomplishments that have been handled by you so successfully. The Islington Workshops have been changed by you from what were probably the most inefficient workshops in Australia to what today is undoubtedly the most efficient, best equipped, and the best managed workshop in the Southern hemisphere, and to you alone all of that credit is due for this wonderful change.

In that same year, from the rebuilt Islington Workshops, Fred

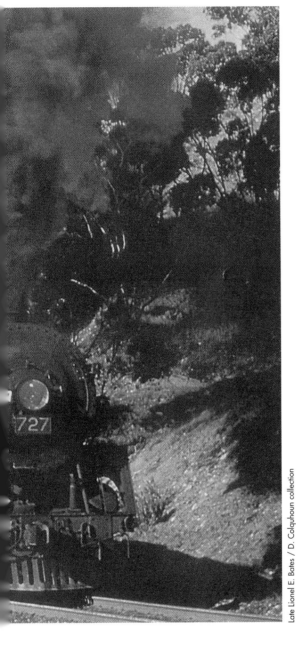

Late Lionel E. Bates / D. Colquhoun collection

completed, as if in a salute to his former chief, a new class of freight locomotive – to the eye, undeniably massive and powerful, and bringing quite a different American-style wheel arrangement to Australian rails, the 2-8-4 Berkshire.

In the U.S., five years previously, designer Will Woodard had introduced the Lima Works' A1 Demonstrator, a new 'super-power' locomotive with a much enlarged firebox (grate area 100 sq ft) supported by a four-wheel trailing truck. The A1 bettered the drawbar horsepower of the best existing Mikado freight engines by 30% and reduced coal consumption by 33%, and within months orders for A1 copies were filling Lima's books. Because initial trials on the Boston and Albany Railroad were held through Massachusetts' steeply-graded Berkshire Hills, this was the generic name that stuck to the bulky 2-8-4, and under the local classification of '720', it was the next type of locomotive that Fred Shea intended for the SAR.

According to the photographer, the late Lionel Bates, Berkshire no. 727 was reduced to 4mph as it heaved a 600-ton freight up the grade at Sleeps Hill. The extra plume of steam indicates that the big 2-8-4's booster is cut in.

The 720 class, built in two batches between 1930 and 1943 totalled 17 locomotives. The first batch of five, numbers 720-4, appeared between November 1930 and the following June, keeping Islington busy at a time of increasing world depression; in contrast Newport's erecting shop was empty for six years. The 725-36 batch appeared from 1938-43: from 1936 all boostered locomotives were identified with a 'B' suffix, hence '500B' and '720B'.

A Works photo depicts the Berkshire's awesome outline. Though wheels, cyclinders and motion were identical with Shea's earlier Islington-built 710 class Mikado, the 'Yankee' eye-catching aspects of the new machine were the large – 'bulging' one might almost call it – boiler, the high-pitched cab and the 12-wheel tender.[2] 'To us, they were then the best and most impressive engines that Islington had produced', recalls W.P.

D. Colquhoun / Lloyd Holmes collection

Refuelling at Mile End, no. 732 of the SAR's second Berkshire batch, built 1938-43, is distinguished from early class members by the skirting applied to the running boards and a 'smoothed' boiler exterior, much in the 'semi-streamlined' style of the 500 class.

(Bill) Holmesby who was a young apprentice in the Erecting Shop, and now retired after a lifetime in the railways.

In praise of South Australia's latest engines, the press noted that they weighed 237 tons, and with booster exerted a tractive effort of 52,000 lbs. The grate measured 59.5 sq ft, though by installation of a 'brick wall' inside the firebox for enhanced combustion, this area was later reduced to 46.8 sq ft. Maximum tender capacity was 9400 gallons of water and 17 tons of coal.[3] The locomotive's integral steel frame, and also that of the tender came from the General Steel Casting Company of Illinois, USA, as did frames of the leading and trailing trucks. Modern components included a Graham White powered sander, a Nathan coal pusher, HT mechanical stoker, air-operated ashpan doors, multiple valve front-end throttle and Ashcroft cut-off control. Nicholson thermic siphons, arch tubes and a combustion chamber were incorporated in the firebox of the large all-steel boiler. Steam pressure at 215 lbs was the highest on the SAR.

The boosters (auxiliary engines) for the four-wheel Delta trailing trucks and the mechanical strokers were originally imported in April 1928

Late Lionel E. Bates / Lloyd Holmes collection

A Tailem Bend-bound freight at Sleeps Hill with no. 734 in charge.

for the existing Pacific and Mikado classes – modifications that either did not proceed or in the case of the 710's boosters, caused problems of excessive axle load. Cost of the 720 back in the 1930s was given at £23,000 each.

Yet for all its size, the 720 was intended to be a versatile 'light line' engine, indeed kinder to the track that a 710 class Mikado. Herein we meet the strange virus of misunderstanding, miscalculation and misadventure that, in one way or another, seems to dog some of Australia's last steam giants. The SAR's Chief Civil Engineer, R. H. Chapman, ruled that Fred's engine, with almost 20 tons on the rear Delta axle, was altogether too big for anything but 80 lb mainline rails, much too weighty for 60 lb branch plant. Further, the 720 could not be operated on certain manual 75 ft branch line turntables.

With the virtue of hindsight, we have to wonder about an engine that is designed in the SAR's own drawing office, presumably with the normal inter-branch conferences; and built in Islington Workshops where each pound of steel can be accounted for – yet emerges far too heavy for the purpose intended! Did Fred go wrong? Did someone not do their sums in Chief Designer Jimmy Hunter's drawing office? In another era, in a more brutal culture, surely heads would roll.

The 720 went into mainline freight and grain haulage, operating over the South to Tailem Bend and beyond, and on the North where Port Pirie would ultimately become accessible to the broad gauge. Behind the scenes, removal of boosters transformed the 710 class into the acceptable 'light liners' that the big Berkshires should have been. Would Boeing design a 747 that could only land at a couple of the world's airports? Would a cruise

D Colquhoun / Lloyd Holmes collection

line introduce a ship that, say, couldn't fit through Sydney Heads? It remains a puzzlement.

The 720 was hard worked to handle record wartime traffic, but plans to add a further three locomotives did not eventuate, with Islington absorbed in production of the Australian Standard Garratt and commencing to build the 520.[4] (Commonwealth cast steel beds intended for numbers 737-9 languished outside the Workshops for almost another 20 years). The smaller driving wheels testified that the Berkshires were not intended for serious passenger duty, though they did work race specials, yet number 725, the first of the second batch, emerged in 1938 wearing the green and silver sheathing that had been applied to the 500 for its *Overland* duty. The 500's smart running board valances were added to the second batch, while in 1949 number 734 had the extended Cyclone front-end fitted, giving the locomotive an undeniably aggressive snout.[5]

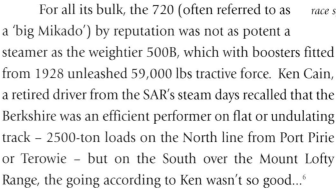
Hooked to a long train of the SAR's wooden suburban cars, Berkshire 722 was caught at 50mph (80kph) on a race special from Gawler.

For all its bulk, the 720 (often referred to as a 'big Mikado') by reputation was not as potent a steamer as the weightier 500B, which with boosters fitted from 1928 unleashed 59,000 lbs tractive force. Ken Cain, a retired driver from the SAR's steam days recalled that the Berkshire was an efficient performer on flat or undulating track – 2500-ton loads on the North line from Port Pirie or Terowie – but on the South over the Mount Lofty Range, the going according to Ken wasn't so good...[6] The south, with its mixture of steep grades and tight curves sometimes appeared too much for the 720, even with the booster cut in. Nor could you leave the booster on for too long, as it made a heavy drain on the 720's steaming capacity and water. But in contrast we had no problems with the older 500 which could take maximum loads over the hills of 500 tons, non-booster, and 540 tons with booster cut in. For the 720 it was 385 tons non-booster and 450 tons with booster working. Even allowing for the difference, it still needed full pressure from the 720's boiler to maintain your schedule. But on the lines to the north of Adelaide it was a better story

where the 720 was good at handling the loads. The Duplex stoker was okay, but the Simplex type had the habit of clogging when large lumps of heavier coal came through.

My crewing of the 720 came in the latter part of the loco's working life when it often had to run with poor quality coal until conversion to oil, and oil-coal combined, which lifted performance. Maintenance was short and some were pretty well worn. So you have to be fair.[7]

Talking of performance, number 724 perhaps typifies the problem of inadequate quality fuel that dogged the SAR post war. The big loco was converted in December 1949 to burning a mixture of Leigh Creek coal and oil, went back to coal in September 1952, to coal-oil again in August 1953, to straight oil in September 1954 and finally returned to coal in April 1957.[8]

South Australian enthusiasts salute the 'nostalgic sight and sound of one of the big 2-8-4s slogging up Mount Lofty with a South line freight, the chatter of the booster sounding through the mighty blast of the main exhaust. Always we will remember those unique machines, the Berkshires.' The late John Buckland recalled photographing a 720, which had a 45mph (72kph) speed limit in a curious role. He captured it lumbering out of Sleeps Hill tunnel on a four-car local weighing all of 120 tons, just about half the loco's own weight.[9]

With dieselisation of the SAR, the 720s were among the first steam to be scrapped.[10] By April 1960 all were 'off the books.' None of them exceeded a million miles – far from it in the instance of those built in 1943.[11] The last no.736 went to the scrapyard with just 411,097 miles (657,759km) on the register. The big Berkshires, South Australia's unique contribution to the Last Giants of the Steam Age, passed into memory.

L. Holmes collection

*Booster-assisted 723
approaching Mount Lofty with
an interstate freight. The year
was 1953 when, despite the
through broad gauge, all
locomotives were changed at the
border with Victoria.*

ODE TO BIG ENGINES

*We have long been out of pocket,
With old engines like the Rocket,
That have jerked and puffed and snorted up the hills.
As for them our love's not votive,
We demand a locomotive,
That will give us decent value for our bills.*

*Rx types are obsolescent,
You can have them for a present,
They'd be handy in a café heating pies.
What we want is power and action,
With a tidy dose of traction,
That will hustle bigger burdens up the rise.*

*Now it seems that the specific,
Is a Mountain or Pacific,
They are types of locos running over sea.
And the vaunted Rx codger,
Ought to haul the Clapham dodger,
Maybe getting Mitcham people home to tea.*

*Oh, the old regime defenders,
Must be sore; the call for tenders,
Will depress their spirits to a lower ebb.
Soon we hope to travel faster,
And we'll have to thank the master,
Who's a certain Yankee fellow known as Webb.*

Seabee, *The Mail*, Adelaide
June 1923.

A 'QR touch' is evident in the brass-bound boiler of the CR's new C class, built in 1937-38 at Walkers Limited, Maryborough, birthplace of hundreds of Queensland locomotives. Otherwise the C was a straight copy of the well-proven C36 of the New South Wales Government Railways.

CHAPTER 3

STANDARD GAUGE 1938 *to* 1957

A MARATHON RUNNER
COMRAILS' C CLASS

Walkers Limited / Author's collection

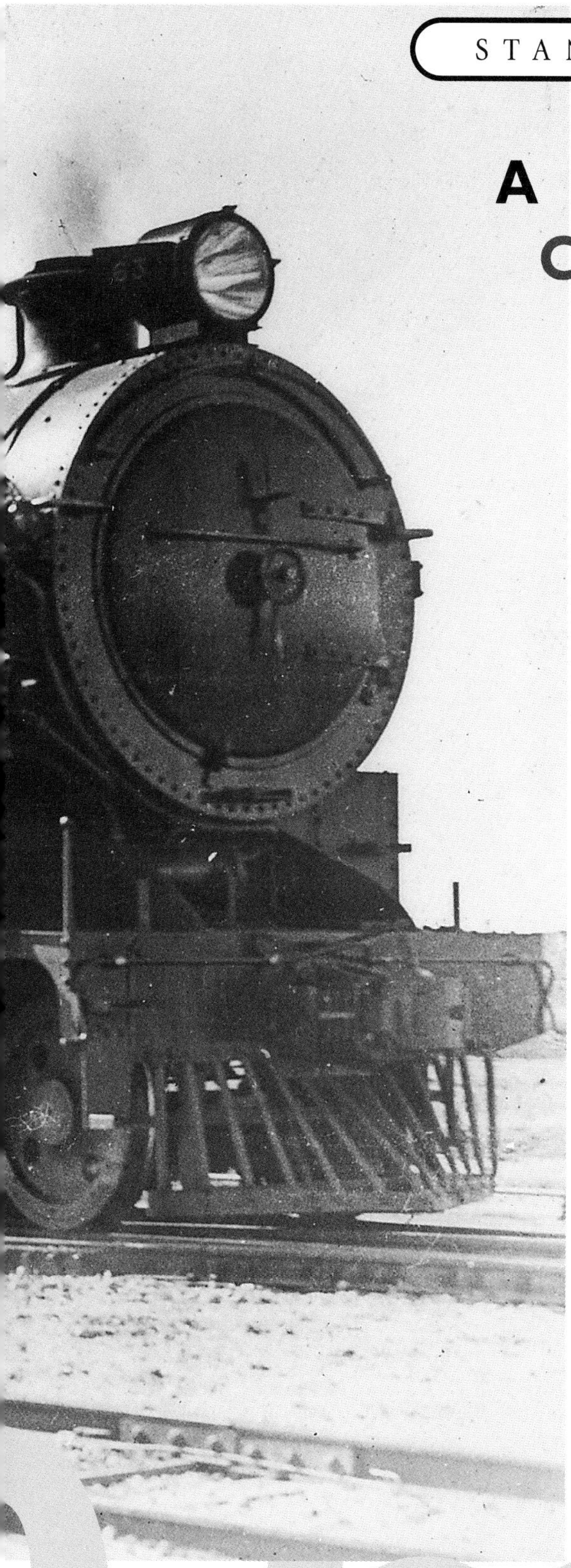

Commonwealth Railways is now only a memory. Some folk probably have never heard of this unique railway organisation begun by the Federal Government to join Australia's east and west.

They have linked the East
where the red suns rise
To the West where the suns go
down;
The steam-exhaust in the
desert dies
As its echoes in silence
drown.[1]

In the 1960s, Australian National Railways took over the Trans-Australian operation, excising all reference to the historic name 'Commonwealth.'

Yet Commonwealth Railways embodied the first great physical work of Federation. Indeed, they were a fulfilment of a vital promise that made Federation complete, helping to bring Western Australia into the union, a tribute to the unceasing campaigning of the strong man of the West, Sir John Forrest.

Built between 1912 and 1917 and never officially opened because of the overshadowing gloom of World War 1, the 'CR' for more than 50 years ran its standard gauge trains for 1051 miles (1682 km) between Port Augusta and Kalgoorlie, across some of the world's most inhospitable terrain.

The *Indian Pacific* streamliner, now privately owned, has replaced the wooden carriages of the Trans-Australian Express. National Rail, together with a covey of transport contractors now run the kilometres-long freights. And 'AN' itself (as it was latterly known) is no more, its short life vaporised at the stroke of a Government pen. Sic transit gloria mundi!

The Trans-Australian line which includes the world's longest straight of 297 miles (475 km) across the Nullarbor Plain has passed to the control of a new government management group, Australian Rail Track Corporation (ARTC). The frustrating gauge breaks at Kalgoorlie and Port Augusta, and then Port Pirie have long ago disappeared under the Federal Government's transcontinental gauge unification program. Just as 'Comrails' (as the cognoscenti knew it) has been erased, so has most of the evidence that the Trans-Australian was once a steam railway, probably one of the world's most difficult to tax the steam engine.

Driver Dugald Durrock's report of G13 back in the construction days encapsulates the ever present problem of trying to raise steam from water that was sometimes more salty than the sea itself. Dugald, with an inspection party train bound for the Western railhead was 45 minutes late out of Hughes because, as he put it, 'Leaky boiler tubes had caused shyness of steam, a result of bad water on the Nullarbor'...

Henry Deane, Engineer-in-Chief during the first phase of Trans-Australian construction. Deane tried to introduce an early diesel locomotive, but in 1913 was forced to settle for the veteran P.6 (C32) class of New South Wales.

Author's collection

Author's collection

After stopping at Cook, I examined my engine to see that all was in order before proceeding into the next section of our journey, I noted an excess of water running from the firebox ashpan. Anticipating that the old enemy – bore water of the Nullarbor Plain – was once again showing its teeth, I mounted the running plate to examine the firebox tubeplate and found on inspection that it was covered with running water, all tubes were leaking at the same time to such an extent that one injector was not maintaining the level of water in the boiler.

Arrival of the first Trans-Australian Express at Kalgoorlie on 24 October 1917.

When the mechanical superintendent advised him that no other locomotive was available, Dugald recalled his experience with an engineman at Falkirk in his native Scotland...

I said, "All right, get me a box full of sawdust from the provision store." "Sawdust!" exclaimed the super, "I have never heard of it! "I assured him that if I got the sawdust asked for I would stop the leaky tubes and then take him and his party to anywhere they wanted to go. The super replied: "If I awake the manager of the store now to give us sawdust, I will have to pay him two hours overtime." Owing to the astonishment exhibited by the superintendent to my suggestion that sawdust be used as a sure means of getting the train through, and his further statement that he would have to pay the store manager two hours overtime, I realised that he did not believe me and was unwilling to put my suggestion to the test, so we got no sawdust. G13 went into the loco shed at Cook and the official party had to travel up the rest of the line by section car.

Eventually Dugald's message reached higher authority and after the appointment of a new superintendent, every locomotive on the east-west carried a pine box full of sawdust shavings for emergency use on the back of the tender.[2]

Henry Deane, first Engineer-in-Chief of construction almost made Trans-Australian history by introducing the world's first long-distance locomotive powered by internal combustion. His 1911 Report showed how the railway could come to grips with a terrain where an average 8-inch rainfall disappeared under a 9ft annual evaporation rate...

> Overseas they are developing combustion engines to the point where they drive heavy ships. If the horsepower can be maintained but the weight factor reduced by 25 per cent, the combustion engine for locomotives would be the answer to our problem which is inseparable from the need of having to tranship heavy tonnages of coal and water for fuel for distances of up to 700 miles.

Deane, who had proposed a Sydney Harbour bridge and electrifying the Blue Mountains line was always thinking ahead, as his Report continued...

> I am informed that attempts are being made to utilise another type of internal combustion engine for this purpose, named the Diesel. In this engine, the oil, which is of the heavier or non-inflammable kind, is forced as a jet into the cylinders with a supply of air under high pressure sufficient

E.E. Lucy who advised Henry Deane on his original choice of steam motive power. As Chief Mechanical Engineer of the NSWGR, Ernest Lucy was responsible for the 1925 introduction of the C36 class express locomotive.

Author's collection

to ignite the same. This class of oil is much safer to use but the engines are heavier and more expensive. The Diesel engine would drive a dynamo, the current from which would be used to give motion to the axles by means of electric motors.

A representative of the British General Electric Company in Sydney advised that his firm is working 'on these lines, and that the outlook is promising'. Deane also understood that that the largest German builders of the Diesel engine, presumably the Maschinen-fabrik

A beflagged G class hauled the inaugural train at the opening of the Commonwealth Railways' extension to Port Pirie on 23 July 1937.

Augsburg, Nurnberg, had a locomotive of this type equipped at their works. He suggested it would be desirable to use one or other of these types during construction...

> so that when the time is ripe for purchasing rolling-stock for the permanent traffic, some valuable experience would have been gained. It is not of much good waiting for other countries to lead the way, as the conditions of the Kalgoorlie-Port Augusta railway are somewhat unique.

The engineering optimists, joined by a spokesman of the McKeen Car Company of America all assured Henry they could supply an engine sufficiently powerful for the Trans-Australian traffic. Before resigning in 1914, Deane in fact came close to ordering from another manufacturer, Hawthorn, Leslie and Company of Newcastle-on-Tyne, a diesel-electric known as the Paragon that, on a 18-ton axle load, promised to take a 300 ton express at 66 mph (107 kph). How far better the Paragon (if it worked!) would have suited the Trans-Australian challenge, but the Chief Engineer's efforts were blunted by the nay-sayers and political meddlers, plus the impact of World War 1.[3] Hoping for a diesel miracle, Deane delayed his locomotive ordering decision until the very last moment and was forced in 1913 into accepting an 'off the shelf' steam design from the country's only other standard gauge rail system (for which he had once worked), that of New South Wales.

Ernest Edward Lucy, Chief Mechanical Engineer of the NSWGR advised in favour of the well-tried P6 class (later reclassified C32) which his predecessor, William Thow had introduced as a new express engine back in 1892. Orders were distributed among a variety of builders, Baldwin of Philadelphia ('delivery in 15 weeks'), Clyde of Sydney and Toowoomba Foundry, Queensland – a testimony to the now urgent need for engines. Under the nomenclature of G class and with the addition of auto couplers and cowcatchers, these unglamorous 10-wheelers dragged the construction trains through the Barton sandhills and rumbled across the Nullarbor's eerie silence.

Rather too late, Deane himself planned a steam locomotive, a high wheeled four-cylinder compound 4-6-0, based on a proposal from Robert Stephenson and Company of England.[4] The first Chief Mechanical Engineer, Malcolm McGregor Henderson went one better and requested funds to design a large 4-6-2 type to be known as H class, weighing 165 tons, with a 41 square foot grate, and on 6ft 8in driving wheels capable of 70 mph (112 kph). This Pacific locomotive would have been quite a Trans-Australian racehorse.

Government timidity ensured that nothing came of these plans. Instead 26 G class went into service between 1914 and 1918. G21 hauled the first Trans-Australian Express from Port Augusta on the night of

CR/Author's collection

22 October, 1917 and, via the labours of nine other G class along the way, they brought the train with its load of VIPs through to a cheering, flag waving crowd at Kalgoorlie 42 hours and 48 minutes later.

But what a Pandora's box of trouble had been sprung as the G class (and the companion K class 2-8-0 freight engines, copies of the NSWGR's Standard Goods) struggled to keep the Transcontinental moving. Not a single running stream, nor any nearby source of useful coal lay throughout the 1051-mile crossing. Along the line, some 240 million litres of water would have to be impounded in asphalt-lined dams. From deep inside

A side-on view of the C class illustrates the size of the immense six-wheel bogie tender, which measured longer than the locomotive itself. With a capacity for 17 tons of coal and 12,000 gallons of water, the loaded tender weighed 120 tons against 87 tons for the locomotive.

Author's collection

Walkers Limited/Author's collection

No. 3601, leader of the NSWGR's C36 class, as delivered by Eveleigh Workshops 1925.

the earth 27 sub-artesian bores produced water impreg-nated with magnesium, calcium and sodium chlorides. Boiler repairs accounted for more than three-quarters of all locomotive main-tenance. A tube plate might last two years, a boiler's life fortunate to be five years. Water hauled over 300 miles (480 km) between depots and New South Wales coal shipped 2000 miles from Newcastle, then trucked another 1000 miles all the way from Port Augusta to Kalgoorlie. Trains could be stranded in the distant silence, waiting for relief. A message from Supervising Engineer Smith at Parkeston Shed (outside Kalgoorlie) typified the problem...

Building a massive C class tender in the shipyard workshops at Walkers Limited, Maryborough. Eight C class were delivered by the Queensland company in 1937-38

> Bad water is giving great trouble on most of the engines, the chief difficulties being priming when steaming, scaling and corrosion.

Boilermakers were reported to be working around the clock to keep engines in steam, shielding themselves with bags inside hot fireboxes. At Port Augusta they took the desperate measure of trying saltwater washouts to defeat the boiler scale. Fitter-in-Charge Forbes telegraphed his boss from Kalgoorlie that G6 was disabled with 50 leaking crown stays. The reply from the CME was 'take whatever action necessary to keep running.'

Author's photograph

The CR enlisted the aid of science but the experts' findings were far from reassuring...

> There is no doubt that the water will give serious trouble if used untreated and altogether satisfactory results cannot be expected from this water even with softenings. Kingoonya, Ooldea, Forrest and Rawlinna water would require double treatment and even after such treatment would still be rather unsatisfactory. On account of the large amount of sodium chloride and other salts, the stops at Hughes and 632 miles cannot be treated satisfactorily.
>
> No commercial method is known for treating the water to eliminate calcium and magnesium chlorides, which exist in excessive quantities. These contain a large amount of nitrates, usually dangerous in boilers on account of decomposition at high temperatures and pressures, which form compounds.
>
> The percentage of boiler repairs to total locomotive repairs was 25 per cent in New South Wales, 28 per cent in South Australia, 36 per cent in West Australia, but on the Trans-Australian it reached 87 per cent. During the past three years the quantity of water used for locomotive purposes had averaged 42,251,000 gallons and of that amount 31,500,000 gallons was of inferior quality.

An 'engine requirements' stop for C63 at Rawlinna. 'Elephant ears' smoke deflectors were applied to the eight C class to improve visibility for the loco crews.

The litany of failures continued until 1928 when Commissioner Norris Bell in his Annual Report would write hopefully that barium carbonate treatment of bore water at Kingoonya and the 632 mile point was proving effective in eliminating harmful incrustating and corrosive elements. 'So successful has been the treatment that there has been very little trouble from leaking tubes or damage to boilers from incrustation and corrosion,' said Commissioner Bell.[5] Three years later the Annual Report mentioned that bore water treatment had led to the elimination of '31 tons of scale-forming deposits and 25 tons of corrosive salts which otherwise would have entered the boilers.'

In 1932-33, the improvements in locomotive performance enabled trials using a single G class to take an express of 10-cars and a brake van from Port Augusta through to Cook and another G class to continue onwards from Cook to Kalgoorlie with intermediate refuelling, rather than engine changes, performed at Tarcoola and Rawlinna.[6] Both were distances in excess of 500 miles (800 km), an operating achievement which not many railways elsewhere would have equalled at the time.

The mammoth job of ballasting the 80lb rails of the Trans-Australian slowly advanced, ridding the journey of much of the swirling clouds of red dust that descended upon passengers, while engine crews took some small comfort from the protection of a louvre-window cab in place of the original ugly and inadequate 'porthole' shelter.

Eventually in July 1937 came the long awaited completion of the standard gauge to link Port Augusta with Port Pirie and joining of the South Australian broad gauge from Adelaide to Port Pirie. The tiresome narrow gauge interlude between Terowie, Quorn and Port Augusta was thus eliminated, enabling Commissioner Gahan to announce in June 1938...

A fast express timetable has come into operation between West Australia and the Eastern States. This saves a day in each direction and is by far the most important change since the commencement of the Trans-Australian line. This has been made possible by the construction of the line to Redhill, the ballasting of the Trans-Australian line, and the introduction of the new locomotives.[7]

The demand for a more powerful locomotive to supplant the G class once again dictated an 'off the shelf' choice in favour of New South Wales' latest express locomotive, the C36. This capable ten-wheeler, with 5ft 9in driving wheels (against 5ft on the G class) had first rolled out of Eveleigh in 1925, under the signature of E E Lucy, though the CME's ambitious deputy, A D J Forster claimed he was the real designer.[8]

In 1936 Walkers Limited of Maryborough, the Queensland company that had delivered some of the CR's K class, secured a contract to build eight locomotives, simply known as 'C class' at a figure of £17,812 each. Running late due to shortage of material, the locomotives were delivered in 1938. Once again auto couplers and cowcatcher, plus extra boiler washout plugs and a roof ventilator for engine crews likely to meet 116 degree F (46°C) temperatures were added to this 'carbon copy' of another railways' design.

The one gesture to originality was the size of the tender. Clyde had originally offered to build the locomotives at about £17,000 each with a tender the size of the NSWGR's D57 class. But Walker's contract called for a massive vehicle that measured longer than the locomotive itself. With a capacity for $17^1/_2$ tons of coal and 12,000 gallons of water, the tenders were carried on two six-wheel bogies. Engine and tender together weighed 209 tons and measured 81 feet overall. Because of size, Walkers assembled the tenders in their shipyard facility rather than the workshop itself.

When the C class faced an early lubrication problem, Fred Shea, CME of the neighbouring South Australian Railways was summoned to suggest a solution to the same troubles that had dogged the Webb era's big engines at their introduction in 1926.[9] Improved grease lubrication resulted and to lessen dust abrasion, metal covers were tried for a time around the slide bars.

In an early addition to rid smoke from entering the cab, 'elephant ears' style smoke deflectors were fitted against the smokestacks. Two engines, numbers 65 and 68 appeared with boiler top cowlings that gave the C class a quasi-streamlined look, or was it, as someone unkindly suggested, more like the result of drawing office doodling? A proposal to name the locomotives after Governors-General and Prime Ministers never proceeded.

The C class could handle 510-ton express loads, untroubled by the 1-in-80 ruling grade of the Trans-Australian, and some 10 hours were cut from the former G class schedule. During the desperate coal shortage months of 1949 and again in mid-1950, up to five of the class were equipped as oil burners with a 3500 gallon (15,900 litre) fuel tank located in the tender bunker space. It was in World War 2 and afterwards as oil-fired that the C class achieved probably the world's longest unbroken regular operation of a single steam locomotive – that of taking the Express through the entire distance between Port Augusta and Kalgoorlie.[10]

The author sampled one of these herculean runs and retains an indelible memory of riding C65's footplate at night between Tarcoola and Kingoonya, watching the headlight stab through utter darkness, and beyond the firebox door hearing the oil burner's pulsating throb.

'I clearly recall the C class locos, oil burning, running through the section Port Augusta to Kalgoorlie; a marathon achievement for a steam locomotive', wrote Keith Smith, the now retired Commissioner and Chairman of the Commonwealth system.[11] Behind the scenes, Eric Adam, his Chief Mechanical Engineer would be spending anxious moments wondering if his hard-working C class could get through.

'By this time (early 1949) the situation had become critical. When the Commonwealth Government asked the Australian Trade Commissioner in New York, in November 1941, to locate eight new mainline locomotives for the T.A.R., they cabled that "the C class 4-6-0's had been overworked to the extent that they were now considered to be unreliable". According to my records, we would by 1949 have run up a further 8 million engine miles, most of which would have been run by the C class.

'During the Second World War, the maximum train speed on the Trans-Australian had been reduced for economic reasons, but when peace was declared, we had to get back as soon as possible on to the 60 mph Express timetables. There was a heavy demand for accommodation on the Trans Line, and the Chief Traffic Manager asked for additional carriages to be attached. We gradually built up the Express from about 400 to 550 tons. These trains were, in effect, a double consist, with two Dining Cars and related Sleeping Cars. In retrospect, I don't know why I agreed to this state of affairs, as the increased demand on the locomotives must have been obvious.

'Another interesting aspect was that in 1943 we had introduced what we called "Through Running". Up to this time, the Trans line had been operated with locomotives being changed at what were roughly the quarter points – Tarcoola, Cook and Rawlinna. This meant that the locomotive which came off a train could be serviced in time to pick up the following train, which was normal on many long distance runs.

'We considered, however, that there would be less trouble with boilers if we avoided the cooling down and heating up involved in these

Author's photograph

stop-overs, and introduced the system under which the same locomotive took the train right across the Trans Line, about 1000 miles each way, through run. To do this, it was necessary to uncouple the loco at the "quarter points", where it would go into the Loco Depot for servicing, crew change, and if coal fired, go under the overhead bin to collect enough fuel for the next quarter. This system worked fairly well. The passengers enjoyed a leg stretch at places the like of which they had not seen before. Our assumption that the boilers would perform better also proved to be correct, but we did introduce a new hazard. For a locomotive to run that distance, across and back without giving trouble, the servicing at Port Augusta had to be really good. Being extremely short of experienced tradesmen did not help.

Crossing at Karonie: C65 waits in the loop while Ka43 comes through with a train of bogie water wagons. Supplying CR steam required shipping coal 2000 miles from New South Wales, then another 1000 miles across the Trans-Australian; water had to be carried for hundreds of miles.

'I can recall many an anxious Friday evening at Port Augusta in those days. Our home was not far from the Railway Station, and at about 7 pm I could hear the locomotive which had brought the Express from Port Pirie (most likely a CN) moving off, and the C class loco shunting on to the train. I knew that the total tonnage of the train and locomotive would be

750 tons. I also knew that if, for any one of a number of possible reasons, the C class loco should fail, there was not one standby engine on the entire 1000 miles of line which could pull that train out of the single line section in one piece.

'In the event of such a failure, we would have to send in the nearest standby, which could be 80 miles away, and then take the train in two halves to the nearest crossing loop, detach the C class, go back and get the rest of the train, join them up and set out again with a locomotive which could not possibly run the Express timetable, let alone pick up any of the considerable time which by then would have been lost. It also meant that a crippled and very scarce C class loco had to be got back to base as soon as possible. Frequent visits to Train Control to check how things were going was just pack drill. Spending the weekend with this possibility constantly in the back of my mind had a bad effect on my tennis.'[12]

Yet the more modern steam locomotive did not remove the costly necessity of treating water and hauling coal and oil to the distant depots at Tarcoola, Cook, Rawlinna and Parkeston. Ever watchful for an alternative form of traction, Commissioner George Gahan in 1945 reported that the CR had completed an investigation 'into the desirability of replacing steam locomotives on the Trans-Australian railway with diesel-electrics.' Tenders were called for two or alternatively four 1000-horsepower diesels, but the initiative came to nothing.

Continuing his advocacy of diesel power, Commissioner Gahan described the burden of operating steam on the Trans-Australian line...

Author's photograph

At least 20 per cent of our total gross tonnage is involved in the hauling of coal and water. Our normal trains gross is 440 tons (excluding the tender) and the weight of the tender loaded with coal and water is 120 tons. If the tender could be eliminated, as would be the case with diesels the gross load hauled could be increased by approximately 27 per cent. Practically the whole of our business is Interstate and, consequently, we are very vulnerable to competition by sea and air, and it is essential if we are to retain our business and give the service which our customers are entitled to expect, that the timetable must be speeded up. Due to the limitation of the axle load imposed by the 80lb rails and to delays inseparable from steam operation on account of coaling, watering and de-ashing very little improvement can be expected with steam power whereas with diesels the present times between Kalgoorlie and Port Pirie would be halved.

Six years later the express duties of the C class were wiped out 'almost overnight' with the delivery of the Clyde-GM diesel-electrics. CR Commissioner Pat Hannaberry and his long-time friend, Fred Shea, now Director of Engineering at Clyde's Granville (NSW) plant were the architects of the motive power revolution, under the orchestration of CME Keith Smith. Ben Chifley, the

Journey of a marathon runner: C65 pauses in 1949 with the Trans-Australian Express 'somewhere on the Nullarbor Plain'. Distinguished by its boiler-top cowling and large fuel oil tank occupying tender bunker space, the locomotive will have covered more than 1000 miles (1600km) before the firebox grows cold. C65 remained in service until 1956.

CR/Author's collection

former loco driver and now Prime Minister of the Commonwealth, attempted to release the dollars for American trade that would allow Clyde to combine with GM's Electro-Motive Division, but the British Government blocked him. The Chifley Labor Government met defeat and it fell to Prime Minister Menzies in the subsequent Liberal Government to obtain the funds necessary for Clyde in designing and importing the equipment necessary to build 11 locomotives of the 1500 hp GM class in which they reduced engine weight to 110 tons and devised a new 6-wheel bogie limiting axle load of $19^1/_2$ tons.

After 40 years, Henry Deane's dream of efficient locomotion independent of coal and water was about to dawn on the Trans-Australian line. Political fortunes dictated that GM1, *Robert Gordon Menzies* made its trial run over CR tracks on 22 September, 1951 and shortly after hauled the first dieselised Express. Running time for steam was halved to under 24 hours, with average speed at 44 mph (71 kph). Operating costs dropped nearly two-thirds and for 47 weary CR steam locomotives, the doomsday bell had rung.

After a four months stand-by, the C class began an unceremonious journey to the Port Augusta scrap line. C69 went first, in January 1952. Five more followed under the oxy torch in February. Though a few were retained for shunting or emergency service in case of floods, the scrapping of C65 in September 1957 meant the end. The giant tenders survived for some years afterwards, the bogies utilised for special purpose loads. Indeed, was it the tender rather than the locomotive itself that earned the C class an entry of distinction in the litany of Steam's Last Giants? No, the C was a marathon runner without compare.

CR/Author's collection

*A series of colourful posters
were devised by some of
Australia's best known graphic
artists to publicise the 1938
acceleration of the east-west
timetable*

A Song of the Ribbons of Rail

*They have linked the East where the red suns rise
To the West where the suns go down;
The steam-exhaust in the desert dies
As its echoes in silence drown.
There are splashes of smoke and shining steel
On the face of nature scrawled,
They're munching a mile-a-minute meal
Where Lindsay's camels crawled.
While the piston-pow'r of the Baldwin strives
Through the din of the day an night,
Linking our loves and linking our lives
To our brothers beyond the Bight.*

Extract from Dryblower's verse in
The Golden West,
December 1917

Assembling the first shipment of the AD60 class in the large erecting shop at Eveleigh in July 1952. Beyer, Peacock sent one of their senior Manchester foremen to assist in supervising the big task.

Sydney Morning Herald

STANDARD GAUGE 1952 *to* 1973

ONE MAN'S GARRATT
THE AD60 CLASS

By mid-1938, Harold Young was a disappointed man. Five years into his appointment as Chief Mechanical Engineer of the New South Wales Government Railways, he had enthusiastically championed the introduction of a high speed Garratt locomotive to haul the Melbourne Express – and lost. It was not the first time, nor would it be the last that the Aberdeen-born engineer had involved his professional judgement in the efficacy of the Garratt design, that of two separate engine units powered from a single boiler.

Ten years previously it had been a different story when Beyer-Peacock and Company of Manchester was considered as the supplier of a double 2-6-2 engine for the steeply inclined Dorrigo line. Directed by his chief, E E Lucy to analyse the proposal he concluded in a report written from the Drawing Office, Eveleigh on 4 April, 1928: 'I am, therefore, unable to make a recommendation in favour of the "Garratt" engine, neither do I consider it necessary at this time to introduce in these railways an articulated locomotive.'[1]

Turning to 1938, the story would be different. In the years between, Harold had been sent abroad in 1936 to examine the latest locomotive developments in Britain, Europe and North America. Foremost in his mind was finding a new engine to replace the C36, a 4-6-0 design of 1925 that as a single engine was no longer equal to peak Melbourne Express loads. As his report of 23 November, 1936 described…

> one of the pressing problems on the New South Wales Railways at the present time is the need to eliminate double heading on a number of fast Inter-state trains. This practice is most uneconomical in locomotive power, as it seldom happens that the full output of the second engine is required. More usually, its presence is only necessary because the load is, perhaps, one and a half times that permitted for a single engine, or even less.

To illustrate the difficulty, Harold noted that in the six month ended 30 June, a total of 290 assistant engines ran a total of 60,375 miles (96,600km) on the Southern line, and this figure applied to Down trains only.[2] In the period, No 3 (the Melbourne Limited) had been assisted 46 times between Sydney and Goulburn, 120 times between Goulburn and Junee and 74 times from Junee to the border.

On his travels, Harold noted the introduction of fast lightweight diesel trains and continued development of multi-cylinder locomotives. Then, in France, Michel Ducluzeau, Chief Mechanical Engineer of the French-influenced Algerian State Railways invited him to join the crew of one of their latest Garratt express locomotives, undergoing trials on the PLM from Paris.

'The works' of no. 6025, stabled at Braodmeadow Depot in August, 1968. Compared to the 23-ton axle load of the D57 and 58 classes, the AD60's axle load of 16 tons made the Beyer-Garratt a very versatile locomotive.

Dale Budd

The imposing 'double-Pacific', built by Societe Franco Belge, of Raismes, was capable of outputting 3600 hp and reputedly could run like the wind. Route diagrams shown to Harold indicated that the track from Algiers to Oran with its 1-in-50 grades and frequent curves had much in common with the Sydney - Cootamundra stretch of the Main South.

The cab ride must have been memorable. Harold stepped down from the Garratt's footplate knowing he had found the solution to hauling the Melbourne Express. On return to Sydney, his Wilson Street design staff began adapting the Algerian engine (which was also standard gauge) to the imperatives of local practice. Under the CME's guiding hand, they changed

Author's collection

the French wheel arrangement to a 'double 4-6-4' and added a mechanical stoker instead of employing two firemen, which might have been fine in Algeria. With a boiler pressure of 250psi, and 70 inch driving wheels, an hour could easily be saved to Albury with a 500-ton train in tow. In M Ducluzeau's summary of the test runs ...

> All these investigations and trials have confirmed the remarkable suitability of the double-Pacific type Beyer-Garratt locomotive for the haulage of heavy trains at high speeds. Their perfect stability should permit the regular attainment of speeds in the neighbourhood of 87-mph (140 kph) without difficulty on heavy, well-laid track. This is the ideal type of locomotive for service on varied and difficult profiles.

Harold submitted his recommendation together with preliminary sketches to the Secretary for Railways on 11 March 1938. Of a locomotive which promised to revolutionise express steam practice in Australia, he concluded...

> I would say that, having studied the question from all angles .. I am of the opinion that a more powerful locomotive for express service is badly needed, and would be economically justified here, and that a 4-6-4 + 4-6-4 Beyer-Garrett locomotive would be an eminently satisfactory design from the point of view of this Branch. I further

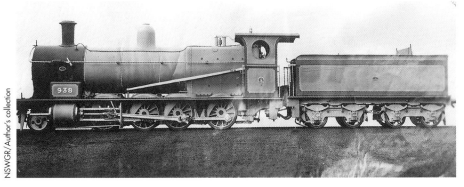

NSWGR/Author's collection

consider that a locomotive of this type would be the most suitable to conform to the engineering and traffic conditions of these Railways.[3]

Anticipating valuable new business for the Manchester works, Beyer, Peacock engaged Rex York, a Sydney businessman as its New South Wales' representative. Alas, the proposal foundered on the desk of the Chief Commissioner, Tom Hartigan. For the Department of Railways it was 'too revolutionary a design' and further, the Beyer-Garratt was 'still in experimental stage as an express locomotive.' Hartigan, incidentally, was an accountant, not an engineer.

With the Garratt consigned to the dusty shelves of rejected designs, the redoubtable Scot switched to the surer ground of a conventional locomotive. Commissioner Hartigan, it is said, would

Top: A Mountain type D57, the NSWGR's first big engine of 1929, on the turntable at Lithgow.

Above: For more than 50 years, the Standard Goods classes, dating from the 1890s, were the work-horses of country freight traffic.

have been satisfied with more C36 ten-wheelers; his CME knew they could do better.

World War 2 intervened and not until 22 January, 1943 did the bullet-nosed 3801 emerge from Clyde Engineering's plant at Granville, and little over a month later made its debut on the Melbourne Express.[4] Clyde built the five 'streamlined' 38 class, while from the Department's own work-shops, Eveleigh contributed 13 and Cardiff 12, bringing the class total to 30. The new Pacific type with its high pressure boiler and wide firebox proved fast, popular and adequate for the job. But did Harold look a trifle wistful at times when he pictured an Algerian Garratt on the Main

Harold Young, Chief Mechanical Engineer of C38 fame, and a key figure in the decision to acquire 50 Beyer-Garratts for the NSWGR. Mr. Young was CME for 28 years, retiring in December 1950.

Below: The famous Algerian Garratt on arrival at Calais Maritime after a high speed run from Paris in 1937.

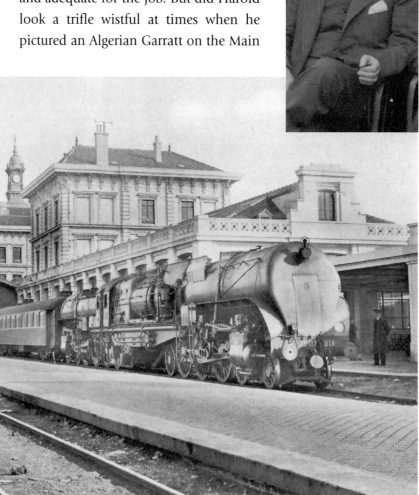

Author's collection

Beyer, Peacock / Author's collection

South rushing through the night?[5]

The production of an express passenger engine was only part of the CME's responsibility. A heavy freight engine to supplement the D57 Mountain class – a 1929 machine which had been Harold's first contribution when promoted to Principal Designing

In the early 1930s, the NSWGR considered introducing its own 2-6-8-0 or 2-8-8-0 Mallet type designs.

Author's collection

Engineer – loomed as an equally pressing challenge.

Work on the new engine was to begin in 1943 but the demands of World War 2 caused serious delays, including the CME's appointment as State Area Controller for Defence Production, when Chullora Workshops were building 500 Beaufort bombers and 250 Beaufighters and assembling heavy tanks. (Recalling those days, his widow, Mrs Dorothy Young, would say of her late husband's work, 'he was one of the unsung heroes of the war.')

The D58 Mountain type freight locomotive, a not-so-successful companion to the earlier D57 class. Only 13 of the proposed 25 locomotives were ever completed.

ARHS Resource Centre

Not until almost five years after peace had been declared did 5801 steam out of Eveleigh on 19 January 1950. Though generally similar to the successful D57, in the few significant changes to the new model, cylinders were smaller and the inside cylinder activated by a change from the Gresley conjugating gear to the CME's own tooth quadrant-and-rack drive, which proved somewhat to be the engine's achilles heel. Only 13 of the proposed D58 order for 25 were ever built.

With the close of the 1940s disturbed and bloody decade, and with only the D58 freight engines in the erecting shops, the NSWGR found itself facing an unenviable moment of truth. Gross ton mileage had climbed 40

In the last days of metropolitan steam, Beyer-Garratt 6009 works a late afternoon freight on the Mascot branch. The order for the AD
powerful Australia's steam age would ever see.

Dale Budd

ass was valued at some £5.2 million. At 265 tons weight and with a 63$^1/_2$ sq ft grate, the locomotives were the largest and most

First Garratt in steam was no. 6002, an object of intense interest to railwaymen when its road trials began in July 1952.

per cent above 1939 levels. Massive new coal mining and other mineral extraction projects were planned across the State, together with an expansion in grain growing. Where was the motive power to handle this increased business? Clearly the shortage of able locomotives had reached crisis point.

On one hand, the large fleet of 2-8-0 Standard Goods engines, a design basically belonging to the 1890s was underpowered for the growing traffic task. On the other, approaching electrification of the major trunk routes from Sydney promised that the Mountain classes would be relieved of much of the heavy haulage (especially coal from the Blue Mountains), yet a D57 or D58 with its 23-ton axle load and limited area of operation (restricted to only 12% of the State system) was exactly what the Railways

Department did not want. Sixty per cent of the system's route mileage still rested on 60 lb (30 kg) rails.

Funds were earmarked to purchase a fleet of electric locomotives for the Blue Mountains, and importation of the first diesel-electrics was contemplated. Yet these engines would be for specific mainline tasks and not available State-wide with the mobility of the veteran 50, 53 and 55 classes and their 16-ton axle loads.[6]

Lack of time demanded some radical decisions. Admittedly, the Garratt design had been rejected four times by the NSWGR. Yet anyone who opened a railway technical journal would recognise the Beyer-Garratt's impressive contribution to the railways of Africa, India, South America and elsewhere, embodying power with light line agility. Nor had the railways themselves entirely spurned the articulated principle, for on two occasions (1931 and 1933) Mallet type proposals utilising D57 boiler and D55 engine frames (making a 2-8-8-0 and 2-6-8-0) had been studied in the drawing office.

Nor did Harold Young seem to have lost his belief in the Garratt's efficiency. Worth remembering is his statement before Justice Wolff's 1946 inquiry into the unsatisfactory record of the Australian Standard Garratt when he declared 'I am of the opinion that the ASG engine fundamentally is quite all right... The general outline is good and basically sound and I see no reason why the engine should not give many years of useful work.'[7]

Urgency called for a major decision on the State's engine power policy. No more time for paper locomotives. No more procrastination. No more frustrated dealings with local manufacturers. The then Acting Transport Minister Billy Sheahan left no one in doubt when he told the Legislative Assembly on 28 April, 1949 that the State Government had been forced to turn to Britain for the supply of 25 locomotives of the Beyer-Garratt articulated type.

On 27 September in the following year he made an intriguing statement to the House on the need to increase the Garratt order...

The railways are extremely short of engine power. About the end of

ARHS Resource Centre

July I was astounded to learn that though approval had been given for the purchase of urgently needed locomotives, the Railway Department had not yet placed an order ... I was informed that the Railways Chief Mechanical Engineer had not yet made up his mind about certain details and that the Railway Commissioner was not disposed to hurry him. Strangely enough, in the quarter of an hour that it took the two gentlemen to come from Railways House in York Street to Martin Place, the Chief Mechanical Engineer succeeded in making up his mind –a condition he had not been able to reach for considerably longer than twelve months.

In June 1949, with a change of Chief Commissionership to F.C. Garside, and Reg Winsor as Assistant Commissioner, Harold Young at last had been able to witness the signing of an order to buy the Beyer-Garratts for New South Wales. The AD60 class, as they were to be known, would be built in the Manchester works of Beyer, Peacock, a company that was an historic engine supplier since colonial days to the railways of New South Wales. They would be the largest and most powerful steam locomotives ever to run on an Australian railway.

Nothing quite like the bulk and length of this 265-ton fat-boilered machine had been seen before on the State's metals. It operated on a pressure of 200 lbs psi and, as originally imported, exerted a tractive effort of 59,000 lbs (v. 28,000 lbs for a Standard Goods). Most importantly, on a 4-8-4 + 4-8-4 wheel arrangement, it exerted an axle load of only 16 tons. For the Traffic Branch it was an engine that could pull anything and, on the NSWGR's 6000 route miles (9600km), go almost anywhere.

Rising forecasts of developments in the mining industry together with other primary and secondary industry expansion soon indicated to the Government that 25 Beyer-Garratts would be insufficient for the haulage tasks stretching far across New South Wales.[8] Faced with this reality and in the aftermath of some none too subtle ministerial prodding, on 22 August, 1950 the Secretary for Railways, Mr S. Nicholas sent Beyer, Peacock's London office the sort of letter every manufacturer hungers to receive...

Dear Sirs,

The Commissioner for Railways hereby confirms the verbal arrangements made with Mr. H. Wilmot, your Chairman and Managing Director, to accept the offer contained in your Managing Director's letter dated 25th July, 1950, to the Hon. W.F. Sheahan,

Minister for Transport, Sydney, to supply an additional twenty-five (25) Beyer Garratt locomotives of the same description, to the same specification, drawings, terms and conditions and at the same price as apply to engines being supplied under the present contract let to you for twenty-five Beyer Garratt locomotives by my letter of acceptance dated 28th April, 1949, as an extension of that contract, less a special concession of quantity of £50,000 sterling distributed over the total as may be suitable to the Commissioner.

The contract is extended as described above to cover a total of 50 locomotives on condition that delivery of the original 25 locomotives ordered will be accelerated so as to complete that number at your works by the end of the first quarter of 1952 (i.e. 7 months ahead of your present obligation), and complete the second lot of 25 locomotives at your works at one per week commencing in the first quarter of 1953 which would be consecutive with your present delivery obligation in respect of the original 25 locomotives.

No additional security need be furnished but the deed of indemnity of £11,500 sterling accompanying the original contract will require to be extended from 30th June, 1953 to 30th September, 1954.

Doubling of the original order for 25 locomotives subsequently brought the total value of the AD60 contract to

Needing all of a 105ft turntable to accommodate its 4-8-4+4-8-4 wheel arrangement, the AD60 sometimes earned the title of 'centipede' or 'trapdoor spider'.

ARHS Resource Centre

some £5.25 million. Two years after the Secretary's letter, the first engines in a seriously late-running delivery schedule, numbers 6001 and 6002 were unloaded at Darling Harbour in 'knocked down' condition and transported to Eveleigh for assembly. The first in steam, no. 6002 began its trials in July 1952 and 6001 followed into service at the end of the month.[9]

The AD60 was not just a Manchester 'off the shelf' machine, but bore significant improvements that Harold Young demanded for New South Wales. Chief among these was an American made one-piece cast steel engine bed with integral cylinders (the first introduced on a Garratt design); others were the mechanical stoker, power reverse, roller bearings and thermic syphons (in the fireboxes of the second 25 batch).

Ironically, the march of time dictated that Harold Young was no longer in authority when the first AD60, to the fanfare of much publicity, ran through its paces. At the end of December, 1950 he had reached retirement age and Bill Armstrong was his successor.[10] Having waited all these years to bring a Garratt into service, Harold was loath to walk away from a program so large and close to his heart. Nor to let the delicate engineering dealings inseparable from the introduction of a major new locomotive fall into possibly inexpert hands. Interestingly, one of the last messages he received in the month before retirement was a cryptic plea (transmitted as a 'Beam Wireless' cablegram) from the British manufacturer, dated 17 November which read…

> Imperative Beyer, Peacock finalises bed design forthwith otherwise seriously delay completion locomotives.

Harold resolved he had to serve the AD60 from the other side of the desk. In 28 years as CME, he naturally had come to know the top executives of Beyer, Peacock, with whom over latter years he had enjoyed close dealings in finalising the AD60 design. His insistence on the U.S.-manufactured cast steel bed, for instance had called for some plain speaking. The principal figures were H. Wilmot, CBE, Chairman and Managing Director of the company, and the Sales Director, Cyril Williams. Another interested figure was Leon Greenberg, Managing Director of Industrial Steels Limited, of Lidcombe which wanted a stake in the locomotive importing business.

In his first year of retirement, Harold wrote a confidential letter to Beyer, Peacock's London head office on 25 July – expressing his concern about the proper handling of the contract, and offering his services as the company's consulting engineer. Industrial Steels had invited the retired CME to join its Board, and thus could position itself into qualifying as the New South Wales agent. So, in 1951, the letters between Harold, Wilmot, Williams and Greenberg began ...

I note that you have joined the Board of Industrial Steels. My congratulations. I am naturally very interested in your reference to our representation in New South Wales. The matter is still under consideration. I cannot say more just now, but when Mr Wilmot – who has been on a quick visit to South Africa - returns early next month, I will show your letter and we will have a talk about it. Your work in connection with the Garratt is, of course, recognised by us, and having been to Australia and studied conditions over a number of years, I can appreciate the difficulties with which you had to contend.[11] – Williams to Young, August 21, 1951

At the end of the month, Greenberg advised Harold of his own meeting with Williams in London and of the 'tremendous interest' aroused in the representation proposal ... 'so much so that he turned on the drinks after what, I thought, was a comparatively chilly beginning and he certainly kept other people waiting for an appointment. In fact I had a little difficulty in getting away'.

No love appeared to be lost between Harold and the State's major private locomotive builder, Clyde Engineering, of Granville. This set of circumstances arose from the

The electric overhead had not reached Blaxland when no. 6002 came through with mechanical stoker working hard to feed the firebox on the Blue Mountains climb.

ARHS Resource Centre

Government's awarding Clyde the first C38 contract without calling tenders, and the Company's subsequent slow delivery (a more than four-year wait for 3801) and a very substantial rise in charges. In his next move, the CME recommended construction of the D58 in the Department's own workshops; and, as if playing tit-for-tat Ray Purves, the Clyde managing director, protested vociferously over the Garratt contract going to Beyer, Peacock without allowing an Australian company the chance to bid.[12]

When at a cocktail party Bart Anderson, the Commissioner's Secretary casually mentioned Clyde's possible participation in the AD60 order, alarm bells started ringing and it was time for Greenberg to do some urgent explaining, which he did in a letter of 6 October ...

> I note that Anderson mentioned Beyer, Peacock to you at the Cocktail Party and doubtless this gave you some concern. However, as I was trying to explain on the telephone, there is quite a normal explanation for this, in that Wilmot wanted me to bring Clyde into the picture by way of having a separate agreement between Clyde and Beyer Peacock, wherein if the firm were asked to build additional Garratts by the Railways in New South Wales, they would only undertake such building through Beyer, Peacock. It would, therefore, also protect Peacock's in case the Railway Department attempted some modifications against their failure without having the approval of Beyer, Peacock.[13]

Clyde had hesitated to finalise a deal with the big steam builder, Greenberg continued, and the outcome depended on how such an arrangement would be viewed by General Motors. For its part, Beyer, Peacock had developed a 'tremendous respect' for the Australian company and realised 'they are on top' – which might have been another way of recognising that Clyde held a trump card in gaining a licence to manufacture the GM (Electro-Motive Division) diesel locomotive in Australia. Already they were supplying the first 11 diesel electrics to the Commonwealth Railways, soon to be followed with 26 for Victoria – hardly a good omen for steam. Greenberg went on to illustrate Beyer, Peacock's strategy to weather the current steam v. diesel contest ...

> They fear the march of the diesel and are naturally anxious to be friends with Clyde. The steps they have taken to "back the horse both ways", as concerns steam and diesel, are rather interesting. For instance they have a 50% share interest in an English Company

called Metropolitan Vickers Beyer Peacock Ltd. which Company build, at their Works, electric locomotives, diesel electric locomotives and gas turbine locomotives.

This is a very clever arrangement as Wilmot explained it to me. For instance, so far as England is concerned, Beyer, Peacocks fight tooth and nail to introduce steam but Metropolitan Vickers are fighting with equal determination, to introduce diesel. As you full well know, tremendous pressure and propaganda goes on with the Railways before tenders are called but once tenders are called and Beyer ,Peacocks see that it is not to be steam then they get right behind Metropolitan Vickers and find thousands of legitimate reasons why, on that particular occasion, the Railways should order diesel. As he puts it, it is the only way.[14]

As from 1 January 1952, Beyer, Peacock announced they would appoint Industrial Steels Ltd. as their New South Wales representative. The official statement noted that Industrial Steels had on their Board and at their service… 'a railway mechanical expert (at present Mr. Harold Young, lately Chief Mechanical Engineer, New South Wales Government Railways). The present agreement shall be firm for three years. In this period of three years the matter shall be reviewed and a continuation of the representation will naturally depend on someone of some standing in railway mechanical matters being at that time available in the service of Industrial Steels Ltd'.

During the three-year period Beyer, Peacock would pay Industrial Steels Ltd. an annual fee of £1,000 (Sterling) per annum, due quarterly in arrears. Reducing the negotiation to a personal level, Williams told Harold in a letter of 2 November…

> You will now know that we have concluded an agreement with Industrial Steels Ltd. for a period of three years, and are very glad to know that you, as a Director of that Company, will be able to give attention to the fifty Beyer-Garratt locomotives which you recommended for purchase by the New South Wales Government Railways. Your initiate interest and connection with the design of these locomotives and specialities insisted upon places you in a very special position for supervising and sweetering their introduction. There are bound to be hurdles to cross introducing a great big engine of this nature with so many new features, and we feel very happy that you will be giving this matter your personal attention.[15]

Most deals require a loser as well as winner. The gentleman in the loser's corner over the AD60 negotiation was Mr R.S. (Rex) York who for 12 years had conducted business on behalf of his Manchester masters from a modest city office in Elizabeth Street. The 'dear Rex' letter of 1 November from Williams advised Rex to make way for 'the official responsible for the recommending of the placing of this order and who has had so much to do with the design and the specialities recommended to be included in these particular locomotives.'

Rex took it on the chin, so to speak, and on 9 November wrote to Harold, congratulating him on his appointment ('you were responsible for the placing of the order and having had so much to do with their design') yet not quite disguising a certain regret ...

> It however came as a great shock to me to learn that my representation was to terminate in seven weeks time. For nearly three years my whole ambition has been to travel on the footplate of these outstanding locomotives as the official representative of Messrs. Beyer, Peacock & Co., and prove to the whole of Australia, in fact to the whole of the world, what a really up-to-date Beyer-Garratt is capable of doing.

> I am firmly convinced that the improvements and unique features you insisted upon in their design will make these engines an outstanding example of what a really modern steam locomotive is capable of doing. The engines will I think, have a profound influence in the design of many future Beyer-Garratts and further, they should be a very forceful reply to the advocates of diesel traction who insist that "dieselisation" is the only solution to all railway traction problems.[16]

At least Mr York had the solace of still receiving his AD60 commission, believed to be £200 per engine, upon delivery. Protocol surrounding the previous CME's appointment as consulting engineer for an order he had personally recommended was a touchy matter. Wilmot had voiced some concern about possible 'outside questioning' of Harold's new role but had been reassured by Greenberg on 6 October that there was no need for concern as Mr Young would not participate in commission payments.

However, would it be expecting too much to anticipate everything running smoothly in the organisation of the Garratt contract? On 23

October, 1951 Harold received a message from Greenberg suggesting some disquiet with the progress at Beyer, Peacock…

It would appear that the delivery of the first Garratt will be well behind schedule and I know that Tully, the (U.K.) Agent General, is very concerned. I would say he is rather cross with Wilmot particularly as the latter is now not prepared to say when the first locomotive will be delivered. Wilmot gives, as one of the reasons, the delay in getting the cast steel beds from America and the changes in design made by Armstrong without informing him. In addition he claims there is tremendous delay by Armstrong insisting on approving each detail drawing.[17]

Six months later, in a cable of 1 April, 1952 Wilmot was able to advise that 'the first N.S.W. big Garratt has been steamed'. Preliminary photographs of the engine leaving the erecting shop were being airmailed, with official photographs to follow. 'I thought you would like to have this right away,' he added. Young reported to Wilmot of a meeting he had organised with Commissioner Keith Fraser, 'a good friend of mine' on 26 February, 1952. He readily agreed to see Mr. Leon Greenberg, our Managing Director, and myself at 12.30 p.m. We both agreed it was a most cordial interview and the following notes will be of interest...

(1)   As New South Wales is a coal mining State, the Commissioner favours steam locomotives and straight electrification with multiple units and electric locomotives.

(2)   As 107 lb. and 80 lb. rails are in short supply, lighter loads for locomotives will be required for many years and for that reason, he is anxiously looking forward to delivery of the Garratts for goods service. When they are in commission, the Alco diesel locomotives now in goods services will be used for passenger operation.

(3)   The slow progress being made in electrifying the Lithgow scheme threatens the Department's ability to cope with progressively increasing traffic on that section. Mr Fraser is happily of the belief that the Garratts will efficiently cover that period, pending completion of electrification.

(4)   It is believed that saturation of railway sections of the electrified area will follow, and to meet the position arrangements are being made to establish a marshalling yard at Wallerawang, 10 miles West of Lithgow. It will be obvious therefore, that when electrification is

achieved, it will depend on the capacity of the Garratts to supply train loads into Wallerawang.

'The Commissioner volunteered information,' Harold continued, 'that to cover all railway projects, the sum of £29 Million was required. Cabinet reduced this amount to £18 Million, consequently adjustments had to be made and schedules modified. No project has been abandoned or cancelled.'

Again, on 20 May, another meeting with Commissioner Fraser was the subject of a letter to Wilmot. Mr Fraser had expressed interest 'in the remarkable work done by Garratt engines on the Rhodesia and Kenya and Uganda Railways. In the case of the former, 6,000 miles per month per engine, including all repairs etc. We gave it our opinion that the N.S.W. design would exceed those figures assuming train mileage was available.' Harold continued ...

> I was pleased to note that the Commissioner is quite willing to co-operate with your proposal to make a colour talkie film. He thinks it is a great idea and agrees to give a chat prior to the first locomotive run when the Minister for Transport, Mr. Sheehan, Mr Reg. Winsor, Director and Mr. Armstrong, C.M.E. along with his principal assistants, will be present at the function.
>
> Mr. Armstrong is keen to get the Garratts into commission in record time, proof of this is to be found in his decision to have the Garratts erected in the Large Erecting Shop at Eveleigh Workshops, Redfern, under the control of Mr. William Sellars, Works Manager. Mr. Sellars is a capable engineer and will give of his best to ensure efficient erection of the Garratts. I am quite sure he will treat your foreman erector with consideration and give him every assistance, also see to it that the photographer gets a fair go to enable him to make a success of that important part of the film taken in the Works.
>
> Mr. Lambert, the railway chief chemist, is in charge of railway photographers. I have spoken to him to-day and he is willing to study the track between Sydney and Lithgow and locate positions where the Garratts will be shown to best advantage in action for the film.[18]

The arrival of the AD60 class certainly caught the attention of the daily press. The *Sydney Morning Herald* of 27 April, 1952 (alongside a headline that millionaire Tommy Manville's eighth wife died in a New York

AD60 class 6015 and 6034 preparing to drag a western ore train over the 1-in-40 grade between Molong and Orange in March 1964. Double-heading Garratts attracted many an enthusiast to the region in the sixties.

car smash) announced the first of the 50 new Garratts were expected in June. 'Assembling First of Fifty New Garratt Locomotives,' was the paper's front-page picture on 15 July.

On 2 August, again on page one, number 6002 was pictured with a 500-ton load passing through Pennant Hills on its trial run between Enfield and Broadmeadow. Commissioner Fraser travelled on the footplate from North Strathfield to Hornsby. Then on 31 August 1952, an inside page picture showed eight-year-old Terry Williams and Graeme Barrett examining 'the chassis' of 6001 during a weekend public display of the first AD60 at number 7 platform, 'Sydney steam station.' Twenty of the 50 locomotives being built 'in Scotland' had now arrived, said the *Herald* of 4 December. 'Four were unloaded at Woolloomooloo yesterday from the steamer Clan Sutherland; six were already in service with another 10 under assembly.'

Inevitably, the dark clouds of political warfare began to gather.

One wonders if Harold Young knew what lay ahead of him. No longer arrayed with the supreme authority of a CME, he would be left to grapple with a contract coming under increasing attack from numerous unforgiving quarters – from political foes anxious to score points off the Government, and from the enginemen's union opposed to the heat of AD60 cabs, the lack of visibility especially when running bunker first, the danger of suffocation in tight single line tunnels; the men who crewed them coined the terms 'centipedes' or 'trapdoor spiders' to reflect the challenge they faced in operating the huge, bulky locomotives. Hostility too, from local manufacturers aggressively promoting the virtues of diesel over steam, already demonstrated in the Canadian Alco 40 class, which had entered service.

In the end, after much argument and agonising, the AD60 order would be reduced to 42 working locomotives, with the addition of another five in 'knocked down' condition for spare parts, and three totally cancelled. The *Sun-Herald* of 5 October reported a statement by Mr A.W. McNamara, MLC, State President of the Australian Workers' Union, that Railways Commissioner Winsor had informed his Union that 'all overseas and Australian contracts for rolling stock and equipment had been cancelled, or were in the course of being cancelled.' Premier Cahill had stressed that the railways must balance their budget this financial year (last year they showed a deficit of £2,850,000). Completion of 50 Garratts by Beyer, Peacock Ltd. was involved, also 40 electric locomotives valued at about £3 million from Metropolitan Vickers Ltd.

Next day's *Herald* continued the story with the 'Railways Department probably not to know for some time how much it will be able to save through contract suspension or cancellation.' In the same column appeared an announcement that a 36-year-old barrister, one by the name of Edward Gough Whitlam, was Labor's choice to contest the Werriwa by-election.

No 6014 climbing the Cowan bank with Standard Goods assistance at the rear.

The next several columns were devoted to the obituary of Melbourne press baron, Sir Keith Murdoch, father of Rupert, a future world press baron.

But for Garratt followers, the *Herald's* front page news of 26 June, 1954 was the blackest – 'NSW Cancels £2 Million Loco Contract.' Negotiations begun during the previous year meant that 25 engines had been cancelled because of (a) a decision to convert from steam to diesel power as soon as possible and (b) the Department's economy campaign. Heavy compensation might be owing to the manufacturers, Beyer, Peacock and Co., of England.

Christmas Eve of 1954 brought the headline 'Huge Saving Over 13 Locomotives.' The Railways Department, said the *Herald*, estimated a saving of £650,878 over part of a contract for 13 Garratts. Under the terms of cancellation, the department would accept delivery of five locomotives and five sets of spare parts, for which it would pay £stg807,000 instead of a £stg1,327,703 contractual obligation. 'The reason the contract was varied is that we have enough engines,' explained Mr Wetherell, the Transport Minister.

In the New Year's eve paper, Minister Wetherell told readers that the Government would sell the five surplus Garratts if it received reasonable offers for them. In future the Railways would only order new types of diesel-electric locomotives. An attack on the AD60 contract by Dr L.J. Parr,

Plans to operate no. 6042 at the Forbes Vintage Village in the NSW Central West have not succeeded. Now the big engine stands on an isolated length of track among the weeds.

capped what one might call the new year's ominously adverse publicity. In an interview of January 6 (1955), Dr Parr, the Liberal member for Burwood, accused the Railways Department of failing to write a foolproof contract. He said the Garratts had cost about 50% more than the original contract figure because of alleged rises in the price of labour and materials; yet there was no provision for Department auditors to examine the manufacturer's books. The original contract price for the Garratts signed in November 1949 was £stg54,000 or £A.67,500 per unit, Dr Parr claimed. But when delivered to the department, each locomotive cost about £100,000.

'I don't know that the company (meaning Beyer, Peacock) is a racketeering company as Dr Parr seems to suggest,' Transport Minister Wetherell gave in a rather weakish reply. 'When the order has been completed, the Government will have spent £5,250,000 on the Garratts,' the story concluded.

Eventually the AD60 found their feet on the State's railways. Thirty locomotives were modified with an increase in cylinder diameter and weight redistribution, raising tractive effort to 63,000 lbs and axle load to 18 tons.[19] Initially intended to run feeder services to the mainlines, the power and mobility of the Garratt removed any boundaries from their rostered freight tasks on the north, west and south. Bunker capacity enlarged to 18 tons enabled them to take a 900-ton freight through from Enfield to Goulburn over 1-in-75 grades, and 600 tons across the 1-in-40 between Goulburn and Harden. Various modifications were introduced to improve life on the footplate, and with maturity the enginemen accepted them, sometimes enthusiastically. 'Centipede' and 'trapdoor spider' became expressions of affection.

In his recollection of running the Garratts, the late Michael Robinson described four occasions when standing at the throttle of an AD60 filled him with pride...

'The Garratts were splendid riding machines because of the way the cab, as part of the boiler section, was slung between front and rear engine units. The AD60 was noisy, sure. The rumble of the exhaust, safety valves blowing off, the hiss of the stoker steam-jets all filled the cab. It was like being on a volcano in motion. You knew the Garratt was going fast when they gave you 'tit wobble'. Above 45 mph, nearing their maximum permitted 50, the 'floating ride' of the footplate was such that they made a man's chest sort of move around. That's why we called them the 'tit

Author's photograph

wobblers' - then you know you were moving fast.

'One of my best memories is when we had 1150 tons, a full timetable load. It was along the Dora Creek-Morisset section, off Hawkmount. We were pulled up on a curve at the bottom of the grade. With all those tons behind, could we ever pick up from here? I opened the regulator, wondering. The Garratt ever so slowly began to move ... slowly ... deliberately ... never losing her feet. Then gradually we surged ahead lifting that train right up the hill. I'll never forget that awesome display of power. I blew the whistle in triumph. The memory of that moment often returns to me. When I'm feeling 'low', it still gives me a lift.

'Another time we had to take one of the last Garratts that had received a major overhaul at Eveleigh back to Broadmeadow. We were supposed to go north in the early hours, but they found some local jobs for us. We were much delayed and didn't get going, up the electrified North Suburban line, until the middle of the peak hour. I'll never forget the look on people's faces as we came charging up the bank beyond Ryde. Business people and school kids waiting to catch the morning electrics to town. And us thundering up the line with this enormous glistening steam locomotive that they'd rarely seen before, if ever, because steam was on the way out in Sydney, especially on the electrified Short North, where Garratts normally didn't come south of Gosford. They just walked to the side of the platform and watched us, some of them sort of open mouthed. Some giving a wave and a cheer as that great shining black Garratt went pounding through. It was good to be on an AD60 that morning.

Amid tall grass in a paddock at Forbes stands no. 6042, a once powerful member of the AD60 class. The isolated sections of track belong to a local Vintage Village.

'Then there was that weekend we were in Broadmeadow after a passenger run. Following a lay-over they booked us to go home 'passenger.' My driver was an express man and there didn't seem to be a job for us to take back. But if we could maybe get a goods and at the weekend, much better for our pockets! After waiting in barracks, we went to the roster clerk over at Port Waratah. 'Yes', he said, 'there is a run needing a crew'. Then he looked at us sort of mischievously and added 'but it's a Garratt'. Before my driver could say 'forget it', I spoke up. 'Yeah, we'll take it'. Once we were away from the office my mate said, 'Mike, I've never been on a Garratt in my life. I'm an Eveleigh passenger man, and out of Port Waratah I don't think I even know the road'. I told him to leave it all to me. I'd passed on Garratts. I was an old 'Broady' man and I knew Port Waratah blindfold. Well, we made it. The AD60 performed beautifully and once my mate settled down, he seemed quite at home. He must have been because, old and experienced big wheel man that he was, when we climbed off the footplate in Sydney he stood back and gazed at the engine. 'Mate,' he said, 'it was well worth waiting in barracks. That's a run I'll never forget.'[20]

By January 1957 all 42 Garratts were in service. Their brief but active running life averaged not much more than 15 years, until increasing dieselisation in the late 'sixties and early 'seventies sounded the death knell.[21] Most travelled was 6029, reaching 627,015 miles – close to a million kilometres – when withdrawn in September 1972. Last to go was 6042, given an official send-off to the graveyard in March 1973; after 118 years, it was reputedly the last steam locomotive in government service.

Politicians' florid phrases on the alleged wrongs and failures of the AD60 are buried somewhere in the Hansards of Macquarie Street. The old enginemen's union, once so opposed to the Garratts, has disappeared in a multi-union merger. The Alco 40 class, introduced six months before the first Garratt, failed to outlast the steam locomotives over which they were brandishing their diesel-electric superiority. Beyer, Peacock, a business too tied to the steam age, closed its doors in 1965. Harold Young died in Switzerland, aged 98, on 9 December 1983. And in Canberra, in the care of the Australian Railway Historical Society's A.C.T. Division, Beyer-Garratt 6029 is waiting for a comeback.

Thus survives a Last Giant of Steam.

WHEN STEAM WAS KING

But after the fires are dead and drawn,
And the boiler tubes are cold;
With a fleeting smile we'll think again
Of the glorious days of old.
When we heard the sharp shrill whistle sound,
And felt the smoke drift by.
 Those golden days when steam was king -
Such memories cannot die.

 Ron Longland, published by ARHS (A.C.T.)

In the care of the
ARHS (A.C.T.
Division) no. 6029 is
at the Canberra Rail
Museum 'awaiting a
come-back.'

Author's photograph

THE GRAIN TRAINS ARE ROLLING

Driver Crean tugged the whistle cord. Australia's biggest locomotive sent its deep throated chime echoing across the paddocks.

He grasped the throttle lever. Steam surged around the cylinders. Black smoke gushed from the squat stack. He pulled harder on the lever. From somewhere deep inside the boiler came a noise like thunder as the 16 mighty driving wheels of Garratt 6017 took hold.

So it began – from a siding at Goulburn one morning this week – the long haul of 1,000 tons of wheat destined for Red China's famine-stricken millions. Garratt 6017 on north-bound goods No. 688 (7.30 a.m.) ex Goulburn; gross load 1,471 tons, it was only one of hundreds of wheat trains moving across the tracks in New South Wales.

Only one of hundreds racing to country stores and seaboard silos with the golden grain; only one of many on which engine crews, working long hours of overtime, are earning fortnightly pay cheques of up to £100 and more. Garratt 6017 is a monster. Measuring 104ft from buffer to buffer (the "centipede" or the "trapdoor spider" to the crew), 260 tons of steel rest on all 32 wheels. Eighteen tons of coal are stored in the bunker aft; 9,500 gallons of water in the dual tanks.

The tight box of the cab is cramped with the four of us aboard: Pat Crean, from Enfield, 18 years a driver; Senior Loco. Inspector Mark Roebuck, 40 years on the job; fireman Malcolm Hadson, 23, dark haired and slight, a car-racing enthusiast, from Goulburn. He won't touch a shovel on this trip.

Beneath the Garratt's articulated frame a mechanical stoker is at work, its long screw winding coal into the enormous firebox, jets of steam spraying the lumps across a grate which in area is larger than many a bathroom.

Hauling this year's 78-million bushel harvest – the biggest since 1949 – is a lesson in smooth organisation. Blocks of high-sided hopper waggons are hurrying across the State with express-train precision. Our destination is Rozelle – and the boat for China. The wheat has to be unloaded by 4 p.m.; the trucks on the way back to the country by 5 p.m.

Like a Vesuvius in fiery eruption, Garratt 6017 blasts its way through the quiet bush around Moss Vale. Driver Crean knocks the throttle open wider and winds the valves towards mid-gear to extract the last ounce of push from every pound of superheated steam. Through Bowral and Mittagong the exhaust beats into a steady rhythm. The cab begins to sway.

Some 40,000 bushels are strung out on the train that snakes for almost a quarter of a mile behind us. Loaded from the far flung fields of Temora, and the branch lines out of Cootamundra, the wheat is worth nearly £25,000 – wealth on which Farmers Smith, Brown and Jones have pinned their hopes.

Crean's strong hand darts from throttle to brake, and he nods to the comforting hiss of the compressed air on the long 1-in-75 descent. Rolling the heavy freight is the engineman's art – careful not to snap the couplings at that critical moment when the train is half over a hump and 700 tons hang in one direction, 700 tons in the other.

We gain momentum. The brakes sigh. Speed drops from 38 to a snail-like 15. Mark Roebuck says a big train like this takes half-a-mile to stop at speed. "We've to take it easy," he explains. "If he lets the air drain from the main reservoir there'd be no holding us on a downgrade once we got away."

The Douglas Park hill is the last big incline before Sydney. As luck has it a signal brings us to a halt at the foot of the incline. When, at last, the red arm lowers, Garratt 6017 is fuming like the witches' cauldron. Inside the mammoth boiler, 50 gallons of water every minute are being turned into steam. The gauge teeters on 200lb per square inch.

"Don't worry, we'll eat it," says our Driver. "These Garratts are great locos. Fair terrors when we first got them. Now they've been modified they'll never let you down."

Soon he is leaning his weight on the steel shaft of the throttle. Pistons thrashing into a solid blur, 6017 charges the bank. A hundred pairs of couplers are groaning with the gargantuan pull ... 204 pairs of wheels dancing over the rail joints ... a great plume of smoke and steam rising in our wake ... every deafening blast from the stack and every turn of the connecting rods transmitted to the footplate with a bone-shaking shudder.

Steam in its twilight on the N.S.W.G.R. moves with magnificent splendour still emitting a display of pyrotechnics that are not easily forgotten. The buzzing diesel makes no similar impression.

Puffing, wheezing, clanking, 6017 is the embodiment of something alive as with a final, straining "huff" it heaves us across the summit. Mark Roebuck wipes a coal stained face. "We're bringing home the sheaves," he smiles. "We're bringing in the sheaves...."

A feature by the author in the *Sun-Herald,* 1958

In the

CHAPTER 5

WHERE GIANTS SLEPT
Driving in the lunch hour – the author remembers

We called it 'the Hub of the Universe' and sometimes 'the black hole of Calcutta' – the smoky, steamy heart of Melbourne where action never ceased and noise was the din of a thousand demons at play. I can recall no more dramatic moments in my youthful life than early morning or late afternoon when dozens of engines were 'calling for the road' at North Melbourne Locomotive Depot.

Changing a C class side-rod beside C turntable at North Loco. Old-time railwaymen cautioned, 'if you can lift it, then it's not strong enough'.

VR/Dept of Infrastructure

The pant of Westinghouse pumps brought to life; the rising whir of the turbo-generator; the blast of three short chime whistles calling for the turntable. Then the hiss of escaping steam from cylinder cocks; the 'ker-lunk' of the front bogie wheels dropping to the turntable rails, the grind of the turntable's electric motor straining to aim its burden for mainline or just humble shunting. And all this drama contained within an 1880s-era cavernous brick and iron structure – forever smoke and steam filled, surely the VR's nearest approach to a Dante's Inferno.

To imagine that North Melbourne Loco, where I once worked, should one day cease to exist, that the A, B and C tables would vanish from the earth: in the mid 1940s, in the days of H220, the X, the C and A2, for those who knew it and worked in it, would be to think the impossible!

We had 160 locomotives shedded at North Melbourne. They were of every class, age and power. From No. 174, the lone, tiny washout F class motor of 'Deepdene Dasher' fame to the 260-ton bulk of North Loco's real giant, known to the public as 'Heavy Harry'. We had old T classes 92 and 94, veteran 0-6-0 types that assaulted the coal stage grade each day with a string of loaded wagons in a scary display of pint-sized power. We had the E and Y and classic D4, all with wheels and motion modestly clad behind the shunters' footboards. They awaited despatch to Melbourne Yard, to Port Melbourne, Spotswood, Sunshine, Flemington and every other section of the metropolitan network where trains were to be made up or taken apart. We had ample middle range power: the D3 and even a few D2 survivors without electric headlights; the K and one of my favorites, the long-framed N. Number 110 was the lone booster-equipped member of its class. N111 was known as 'Lord Nelson' – one eye, one arm, one ambition. We had the chunky C class, the largest loco allowed on A or B table. And out on the 'Burma Roads', that roofed-over extension at the rear of the main shed, lurked the heavy X class, known as the 'Night Owls'. By day they seemed to stand idle but when darkness fell and the big freights were

VR/Author's collection

'North Loco' was demolished in January 1965, leaving not a trace of the great Melbourne depot that could daily dispatch 160 locomotives into VR service and knew the comings and goings of more than 700 railwaymen at all hours of the day and night.

put together, the booster equipped X took over with the sound from its hollow throated blastpipe receding into the darkness. We also had, of course, the 'big fella', the lone 4-8-4 goliath, H220. Like the X, it was another phantom of the night, reaching North Loco on a Down trip with a North-East freight during the afternoon, then standing over the pit until its evening departure. The one engine we did not boast was the classic S class, the *Spirit of Progress* locomotives for which Seymour was home depot.

How could one forget the A2? Whether of Stephenson or Walschaert valve gear, the memorable A2 was in many ways the motive power heart of North Loco. We sent them out on the fast morning passengers to Geelong, Ballarat, Bendigo and Bairnsdale. No. 973, with the ACFI feedwater heater, always reserved for the morning's Geelong *Flyer* ('45 miles in 55 minutes'). The A2 Ballast trains, the middle of the night paper trains, the Saturday afternoon to Whittlesea mixed, nothing was beyond the scope of this able and beautiful high-wheel locomotive.

Remember the brace of A2 rushed into service mid-afternoon when an S class had failed (not an unusual situation) to head the Albury Express, 4.15 out of Spencer Street. And a regular night assignment, one to recall best of all, when the two A2s, usually Walschaert engines, were booked on the *Overland*. Two A2s to confront the Ingliston bank and drag that long train of wooden bodied six-wheel bogie cars to Ballarat, Ararat and on to the border. Young firemen talked in subdued tones of their first trip on a double-headed *Overland*, of trying to keep their feet at speed on a shuddering footplate, of the unrelenting firing needed to conquer the infamous Ingliston grade. There was one legendary place, I don't quite know where but if the fireman on the train engine could read the number plate on the rear of the lead engine's tender as they rounded a certain curve, then speed was judged to be approaching the supersonic. North Melbourne had no lack of such loco lore.

Then there were the names of some of the enginemen of yesteryear. Within recall: 'Bull and Bell on the Ballarat Banker', somehow all those 'Bs' are engraved in one's memory. We had 'big wheel' drivers, young drivers, scallywag drivers, taciturn drivers, but among them all I cannot recall a man I did not youthfully admire. What of express driver Wally White, a hefty handsome man whose overalls were carefully laundered and pressed, his jacket and cap forever immaculate and always wore goggles on the footplate. Wally owned a large American car (remember, this is an engineman driving a shiny American car in the 1940s) and was reputed, scandal of scandals, to have a wealthy lady friend!

How fortunate to be observer of life at North Melbourne. Not only an observer but a participant in the heady, steamy days of the 1940s when it seemed that North Loco and its hoard of black engines would go on forever.

Author's collection

Beside North Melbourne's C table, a Walschaert valve gear A2 is prepared for road trials prior to the modified front end conversion program of 1934.

From Newport came the latest steel-boilered K and X classes; the Y class was modified with wide flangeless central driving wheels to take over the coal stage push-up and became 'the steamroller'; 'Polly' the busybody loco crane visited us from the nearby carriage workshops; coal shortages forced the use of firewood on the E class shunters and at night they emitted a shower of sparks equalling any present-day fireworks display. And sadness for the young cleaner who died when his head jammed between an A2 window and the timbers of the coal stage.

I began in the VR as a boy of about 15 or 16. My first job was at Jolimont electric car sheds, introduced to railway life on the end of a broom sweeping up shavings and fetching lunches for the armature-rewinding floor. What a way to run a railway! I graduated to tradesman's helper, crouched beneath the body of M type carriages as, on creaking trestles, they were lowered above our heads by the gantry crane, our job to clean the electrical equipment hidden within those mysterious boxes beneath the carriage floor.

Author's collection

Department of Infrastructure

Employed in similar grade today, no doubt one would be a 'junior executive management trainee' or some such dignified appellation. But I was inducted into the grim and no-nonsense discipline of the railway as a 'junior supernumerary lad labourer'. Just ponder those words: 'junior' - much less than mature; 'supernumerary' - excess baggage, not really needed; 'lad' - not a candidate for responsibility or promotion; and 'labourer', one word that needs no embellishment. But at least I had pull. An uncle by marriage was a Mr Watkins who had a large butcher's shop at the top of Bourke Street and lots of cattleyards and, I believe, booked lots of VR cattle trucks. He was a friend of Commissioner Mick Canny. So within a few months of starting at Jolimont, I was suddenly transferred to my heart's desire, North Melbourne Locomotive Depot. Paradise enow!

In its latter years, 'North Loco' (left) housed Victoria's last express steam power, the 4-6-4 R class, built by North British of Glasgow, from 1951-54.

Above: Locomotive cleaning was the first rung of the ladder in an engineman's life. An unmodified C class 2-8-0 is the subject of attention in the shaddowy depths of North Melbourne shed.

Assistant to the Sign-on Clerk was the first job. Engine crews appeared for duty at his little glass window, at the end of the wind-swept footbridge that led from North Melbourne station. He signed them off again as they emerged from the sooty depths of the shed, grimy and weary, at the

VR dept of Infrastructure

end of their run. We worked three shifts: 7 am, 2 pm and 11 pm starting times. My own job, apart from brewing tea and keeping the fire going was to answer the phone in my little cubicle, and from a list of engine numbers, direct the incoming crews with such arcane commands as 'Shed fire, Maitland' or 'All out washout, Burma Roads'. These were the cryptic messages which told the knights of the footplate where and how to stable their iron steeds.

'Polly', a diminutive crane loco bustled around North Melbourne Shed in the busy days of steam.

Saturdays, the 11 pm was a special shift. One might be a Junior Supernumerary Lad Labourer, but that didn't hinder the VR from appointing you in sole charge of this wondrous locomotive shed, with its scores of priceless steam engines under your supreme control. Perhaps at the flick of a finger you could have despatched a D3 to Nyora, an A2 to Mildura and N110 to Yarram or heaven knows where. Well, a boy might dream. That is, until 7 am Sunday when welcome relief arrived.

I guess it goes without saying that not much happened at North Loco after 11 pm Saturday, at least not enough to justify the rostering of a more highly paid staff. But we did have our moments. I remember one night, with all our engines safely put to bed, when I forgot to dispatch our only stand-by crew – sneaky blokes had persuaded me to sign them off early –

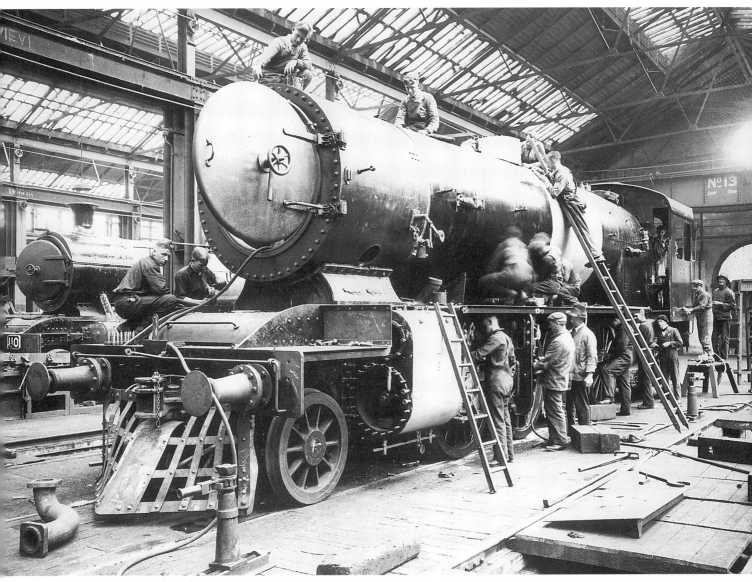

Author's collection

to relieve a ballast job which had been working since mid-afternoon. When the forgotten crew finally returned at 3 am, a barricaded office was the safest way of avoiding the indignity of a punch in the mouth by a very, very, angry driver.

Upwards of 700 men worked at North Loco, always a coming and going on shifts; engine crews, fitters, boilermakers, helpers and so forth. Two distinct societies inhabited the shed; first, the enginemen and all who went with them – hostlers, lighters up, coal heavers, ash pit workers, turntable hands, cleaners. Their instructions came

Newport Workshops were the cradle where most of North Melbourne's locomotive tradesmen mastered their steam skills. Building an N class 2-8-2 at Newport typified the work that led from apprenticeship to expert fitter or boilermaker.

VR/author's collection

from the Shed Foreman who chalked engine numbers on a large blackboard outside his office close by B table. Grouped around C table, the other society belonged to the Foreman Mechanic's domain. To this other world of tradesmen I was suddenly transferred to become a day worker, charged with keeping loco mileage figures and transmitting commands to outstations to 'red oil' certain engines, or send them in for A, B, C or D exams, communicating in the 'zoko waxy wary' lingo of VR telegraphic shorthand.

The Foreman Mechanic's door opened to admit many a memorable man of VR steam years. Ruddy-faced Jack Cornish, Chief Loco Foreman; Bull Holmes, Foreman Mechanic; Jack Doherty, senior Shed Foreman; Fred and George Hartley, Loco Inspectors; and a very dapper George Brown, the youthful Superintendent of Loco Maintenance, launched on a career path that would lead to the heights of Commissionership.

One incident of a major freight derailment involving an X class on the 'pleurisy plains' of the Gheringhap-Maroona line is not easy to forget. North Loco sent out its 60-ton wrecking crane and Bull Holmes went with it to supervise rerailing operations. Another mishap unfortunately intervened. The crane overturned, went down the embankment into the dirt. I can still picture the day when Bull returned to North Loco. He was a muscular, gravel-voiced, decisive man, yet he came into the office as a shamefaced schoolboy; later I overheard Jack Cornish tell someone confidentially that 'never again was Bull Holmes to be sent out to supervise a wreck recovery.'

Many of the clerical assistants were veteran loco men, some with a leg or an arm missing; they could recall the 'Overarmers' and 'Buzzwinkers', the V class compound, the swift

The life of the loco sheds revolved about the men who crewed the engines – this VR driver awaits a departure on an X class from the 'Burma roads'; the stencilled 'N' indicates home depot is North Melbourne.

Author's collection

Up to 160 locomotives were daily dispatched from North Melbourne. No. 981 of the Walschaert A2 class on the morning Bendigo train was one of them.

Lloyd Holmes

AAs and the Belgian Rs. Steam filled the whole atmosphere of North Loco – the talk, the memories, the funny stories, the characters and day-to-day incidents. Part of the legend was 'Black Thursday', that one day of the year on Easter eve when North Loco's resources were taxed to the limit in pushing out sufficient A2s and Cs and any other engines available for the holiday traveller. Unreal days, of course, when the railways knew or cared little for competition from road or air.

Could a growing-up teenager ask for a more memorable environment? Sooty, swearing, deafening, unforgettable. What other young blokes enjoyed the opportunity in their lunch break to drive a big C class or an express A2 around the depot yards, thanks to friendly hostlers; or being called out one night to help a lone fitter in re-railing an X class with a pony truck on the ballast in the depths of Melbourne Yard; and, of course, being in sole charge of the 'Hub of the Universe', if only in the early hours of the Sabbath morn.

To one who knew it, how unthinkable that all this has gone. Quite an emotional moment when one looks from the window of a passing Sydney-bound train and of memorable North Loco, sees not a brick upon a brick.

Grooming an engine began in the sheds and continued 'on the road' where steam demanded the personal attention of its crews. Years of experience are evident as driver Bert Baker applies an oil can to the siderods of H220 on the North East fast goods roster.

Old Steam Locomotives

Retired, they huddle, side-tracked by a field –
Giants, who hurtled gamely through the night,
Building the mammoth sinews of the land,
Opening vistas - mountain brow and canyon.
Their urgent whistles plumbed the echoing cloud;
Deep-mouthed, their bells, importunately clanging.
Now they crouch in monstrous silence, waiting,
Where mallows, buttercups, and daisies blow
In little winds about the cindered siding.

Bertha Wilcox Smith
Originally in THE ROTARIAN

CHAPTER 6

NARROW GAUGE 1922 *to* 1964

THE MAIL ENGINE
QUEENSLAND'S C19

Spit n' polish for both engines and train crew as a decorated no. 700 is readied for service in the State's centenary; the locomotive was also assigned to Royal Train duty in 1934.

QR Historical Centre

The schoolboy waited in the darkness on Bundaberg platform, watching for the beam of an electric headlight to sweep through the trees. A shrill whistle for the Walker Street crossing, the headlamp dimmed, the sigh of Westinghouse brakes, the slowing procession of sleeping cars, with cabins all dark and mysterious. Heady stuff.

Eleven o'clock was late to be out and about, waiting for the Townsville Mail, but on this hot Queensland night a schoolboy could be excused,

QR Historical Centre

no one slept much anyhow. Besides it was number 800 (or possibly 801, both shedded at Maryborough) – what the newspapers called the most powerful locomotive on the Queensland Railways. That was the drawcard.

As it eased into the station, he would glimpse the big boiler, brass bound and glinting, feel a wave of heat from the huge firebox, hear the turbo generator's hum and see the crew in a cab lit by the glow of electric lamps. Worth the wait. Other features would be more familiar, the long-snouted steel cowcatcher, the boiler-mounted sand dome and the four-wheel leading bogie – all of them for their antecedents reaching back to the imported Yankees of the 1880's; and the cutaway cab that reminded him of a latter day B13, arguably the first locomotive to have the special 'Queensland' look.

Yet while the B13 was a puny 50-ton engine of some 10,000 lbs tractive effort,[1] the C19 loomed so much larger, claiming in that schoolboy's memorable 1928 to rate among the world's largest conventional steam locomotives on the 3ft 6in gauge. One point was fairly certain, with a 9ft 6in throw the C19 carried the longest firebox of any narrow gauge machine.

Years later, Noel Conlon, a retired QR engineman recalled his life on the C19's footplate. 'This was a challenging engine, not the sort of "heave the coal in" job that your average Queensland fireman might come to expect. On the C19, because of the depth and size of the grate (21.37 sq ft) he needed to adopt special firing techniques, for one thing learning to "bounce" the shovel off the firehole door to keep the big engine steaming.'[2]

Behind no. 698, the Sydney Mail pauses near Grandchester during the ascent of the Little Liverpool Range. As the State's most powerful locomotive, the C19 was assigned to hauling the QR's 'flagship train' between Brisbane and the border at Wallangarra

QR Historical Centre

The C19 followed the popular 4-8-0 wheel arrangement; indeed, Queensland would have more of these 12-wheelers than any other narrow gauge State. But the first eight-coupled machines were a group of chunky 2-8-0 'Consolidation' type built for the QR in 1879-1881 and typical of the products that Baldwin of Philadelphia was busily exporting around the world; the J of New South Wales, the V of Victoria and South Australia's O and X was by way of later illustration.

After 1926, the new B18^1/$_4$ Pacific type began to displace the C19 from mainline passenger running, leaving the heavy 4-8-0 to concentrate on freight.

Pioneering a ladder-like colonial railway network far across the outback came at the price of slender metals, many sharp curves and spindly iron or timber trestle bridges. Engineers and draftsmen who staffed the QR's drawing office (an 1880s establishment begun rather in advance of other Australian railways) knew that axle load and wheelbase would be confining factors in the building of every Queensland locomotive; and not only these, but the braking power required in the descent of steep grades and the ability of primitive drawgear to hold a train together.

Adaptability of the four-wheel leading bogie had been well demonstrated by the Americans, first on Baldwin's A12 of 1877, and other 4-4-0s that followed. The lesson was effectively adopted in the 4-6-0 and 4-8-0 wheel arrangements which would become the mainstay of QR motive power for decades ahead. The ten-wheeler B15 of 1889, combined with its PB derivatives, grew into a class of 233 locomotives that knew almost no boundaries on the light rails that 'opened up the country'. The saturated boiler C16, first of the far-ranging 12-wheelers, increased to a stable of 152 locomotives until overtaken numerically by the 223 engines of the superheated C17 class of 1920.

From 1877 when Ipswich Workshops commenced its building program and 1890 when private contracts were let, small boilered engines were the hallmark of the Queensland motive power stable. In a new century, when route mileage climbed towards the 6000-mark, the average tractive effort of QR engines stood at 14,500 lbs.[3] Yet within the limitations of a 10-ton mainline axle load, and tortuous 5-chain curves, the quest for greater power would press the limits set by civil engineers. Of all QR's passenger trains, the Sydney Mail was the flagship, providing a connection south from Brisbane to Australia's major capital city, via a break-of-gauge transfer station at Wallangarra where QR and NSWR metals had met in 1888. The Mail comprised the smartest Queensland rolling stock, with swivelling chairs in the Parlour Car and buffet snacks served by a conductor.

Once sacked for 'impertinence', Charles F. Pemberton was the CME responsible for the construction of the C18 class and modification of the design that produced the C19. He retired in 1921.

QR Historical Centre

From the light engine power of last century, the demands of the Sydney traffic by 1911 moved to the pinnacle of Ipswich's ten-wheel design, the B17 which had 4ft driving wheels and developed a 19,000 lb tractive effort. This machine of inelegant proportions commanded the Mail until 1914 when the QR's first 'heavy' engine of close on 100 tons weight was about to enter the scene.

The genesis of the C19 can be attributed to two eminent Queensland railwaymen, Norris Bell – later the builder of the Trans-Australian Railway – and Charles F. Pemberton, an innovative engineer once sacked for his 'impertinence.'[4]

As Chief (civil) Engineer, Bell agreed that Queensland's growing mainline traffic demanded a locomotive more powerful than the C16, provided the 10-ton axle load could be observed. Pemberton as Chief Mechanical Engineer offered the alternatives of a six-coupled Beyer-Garratt to be known as the 'BB15' (similar to the recently imported Tasmanian L class) or a conventional and trusty 4-8-0. Though the QR had been flirting with the prospect of introducing a Garratt (and would continue to think about it for another 40 years) once again they shied away from going 'articulated.' In effect the decision gave a green light to Pemberton's eight-coupled design; based on cylinder diameter and the number of coupled wheels, the new engine became the C18 – forerunner of the C19.

QR Historical Centre

In November 1911 Commissioner Charles B. Evans authorised the construction of three locomotives that would be able 'to haul 240 tons up the Toowoomba Range at 20 miles per hour.' In 1914 Ipswich Workshops delivered number 692, a saturated boiler machine, while to test the effectiveness of the new trend in Australia towards superheating, 693 appeared with a Schmidt type super-heater and 694 with a Robinson type. The improved steaming performance of the two equipped locomotives was such that in 1916, superheating was also provided to 692.

On the strengthened Southern line, the C18 was assigned to take the

The men who built no. 702, the 100th engine completed at Ispwich Workshops, pose beside their latest C19. The locomotive fittingly received the name Centenary.

10-car Sydney Mail through from Brisbane, up the range to Toowoomba and onwards to the border. Senior drivers from Warwick Shed attached a silvered metal star to the smokebox door to signify the importance of Queensland's biggest locomotive hauling its most prestigious train.

A further recognition of C18 dignity came when Colonel Evans obtained vice-regal approval in 1915 to name two locomotives after the State Governor and his wife – 693 as *Sir Wm MacGregor* ('William' was too long for the nameplate) and 694 as *Lady MacGregor*.[5]

The gradual improvement of the Western and North Coast main lines to 60 lb standard, and the prospect of a link-up at Mackay which eventually would clear the way for a thousand-mile journey from Brisbane to the tropics, needed more heavyweight locomotives. The C18, to quote Pemberton's words, was 'designed to the limit of existing drawgear.' In simple terms, though Garratt inquiries still persisted, this meant that the CME had no latitude to introduce a bigger locomotive, and in view of the trailing load limitations, such a move would seem to be pointless.[6] The solution would be more of the same, more of the C18.

Pemberton retired early at the age of 61 in 1921 – some said to invent (literally) a better mousetrap to combat the western plagues, but this morsel of railway folklore is contested. At any rate, before signing off on a locomotive he would not be in harness to see completed, he and his Chief Draftsman J. H. Rees had a change of plan.[7] Instead of the C18, Pemberton switched the design to a locomotive with 19-inch cylinders, superheated yet otherwise with the same basic dimensions as its predecessor – long firebox to consume Southern Queensland's sub-bitumenous high ash coal, four ft driving wheels on a 12ft 6in wheelbase, but with boiler pressure lowered to 160 lbs psi. Tractive effort was 23,525 lb.

Tenders were called for 35 locomotives; when responses failed to excite, the requirement was reduced to 10 locomotives for construction at Ipswich. Under the direction of Pemberton's successor, John Robinson the first of the C19 class, number 695 began its trials in September 1922, and two years later the delivery of 704 completed the order.[8] Along the way, number 702 appeared in December 1923 as Ipswich Workshops' 100th locomotive. In the following year it was named *Centenary* as part of the celebrations to mark John Oxley's exploration of the Brisbane River.

The centenary also saw the QR's freight business climb to more than five million tons,[9] which resulted in a call on Ipswich to build another 20,

Author's collection

Arrival of the first standard gauge express from Sydney at South Brisbane on 27 September, 1930. The 613-mile (980 km) direct connection reduced the importance of the Wallangarra route.

but reduced to 10 locomotives from 1924-28 at an estimated cost each of £11,800.[10] These engines and those that followed included Robinson's top feed boiler modification and dispensing with Pemberton's large steam dome in favour of a now standard brass regulator dome, modest in size and incorporating the safety valves.

The depression era ushered in an almost 10-year halt in locomotive construction until 1935 when, to coincide with the debut of the new all-roller bearing *Sunshine Express*, Walkers Limited, of Maryborough built a further six locomotives, numbers 196 – 201 which were identified by adoption of the capuchon style smokestack. Because tenders were not called in the cause of State employment, Walkers agreed to limit profit to 10% of this final C19 order.

Rostered regularly on the Sydney Mail, the C19 was the charge of experienced crews who became skilled in handling them on the make or break climb towards Toowoomba. Even so, the locomen's union was not satisfied with the demands of the 97-ton engine or, to be more specific, the appetite of its firebox;[11] calls were made for the total rebuilding, if not scrapping of the C19. Compromises were reached on hours of footplate duty and, as with the introduction of many a new locomotive, the attitude gradually changed to an acceptance, if not a pride in running the big engine.

At 8.05 am, the C19 took the Mail on its 10-hour journey from Brisbane to meet the standard gauge New South Wales express at

Wallangarra. En route it would face a 19-mile ascent of the 2000-ft Main Range, with the nine tunnels and 105 curves and a grade equivalent to 1-in-40. An assisting engine would be rostered to join the 300-ton train between Murphys Creek and Toowoomba, and again between Warwick and the border where at The Summit, near Stanthorpe, elevation reached 3035 ft.[12] Freight loads could approach 600 tons, allowing for assistance on the steep going, a PB on the Range and possibly a C17 on the Southern line. Many an observer, familiar with the wider gauges down south, has been moved to admit 'they might be smaller than our big wheels, but these Queenslanders know how to work their engines like the very devil!'

The Sydney Mail lost its shine with the completion in 1930 of the standard gauge connection, via Kyogle, from South Brisbane to Sydney. From the late 1920s, the new B18$^1/_4$, the QR's first Pacific design and a most successful locomotive began to dominate long distance passenger running.[13] However the C19 was essentially a heavy haul machine and its duty belonged in coal, livestock, grain and express fruit traffic, working the big trains to and from Brisbane across the grades to Rockhampton in the north, Roma to the west, up to an allowable maximum 650 tons as well as their southerly beat.[14]

'We called them the Bulls, or the Big Bulls, because of their size and power,' Noel Conlon recalled in his footplate memories…

They were always a reliable engine and not too tough on water. But like every other Queensland engine, they were thrashed mercilessly during the War, and under wear and tear and lack of maintenance, the plate frames developed cracks which led to binding of the side rods and throwing the valve gear out of true. Repairs were made but welding techniques seemed not up to fixing the problem.

The Southern line in the 1950s saw the C19's last major show on heavy freights. Gradually they were relegated to less demanding rosters around the metropolitan area – on the Cannon Hill stock train you could meet a C19, or shunting the yards at Toowoomba or on the local Willowburn workers' train where they looked not much like the gleaming Mail engines of the 1920s.

Author's collection

One of the named and C18 converted locomotives, now designed at 'CC19', is chosen for the ARHS (Qld Division) annual outings. 'T' on the buffer beam indicates Toowoomba Depot.

From the mid-1950s their days were numbered when the march of the diesels began.[15] George Bond, the schoolboy watcher of Bundaberg nights, an enthusiast for the C19, brought his camera when they put old 800 to the torch. 'My hand shook when I took the picture', said George. 'I felt like crying.'[16]

Survivor of the C19 class, no. 700 (Works no. 98 of 17 August 1923) is stored at the North Ipswich Workshops. No. 700, known to railwaymen as 'Coo-ee', was the locomotive that in December, 1934 drew the special train of the Governor-General, the Duke of Gloucester from Wallangarra to Brisbane and on to Nambour. Written off on 26 February, 1964, this Last Giant retired with 975,450 miles (1,560,720 km) on the clock, and knowing its moment of glory.

On the Queensland Railway Lines

*The QR's first eight-coupled locomotives
were Consolidations imported from Baldwin
of Philadelphia in 1879-81.*

Author's collection

*On the Queensland railway lines
There are stations where one dines;
Private individuals
Also run refreshment stalls.
Chorus:*

*Bogan-Tungan, Rollingstone,
Mungar, Murgon, Marathon(e),
Guthalungra, Pinkenba
Wanko, Yaamba - ha,ha,ha;*

*Pies and coffee, baths and showers
Are supplied at Charters Towers;
At Mackay the rule prevails
Of restricting showers to males.*

*Males and females, high and dry,
Hang around at Durikai,
Boora-Mugga, Djarawong,
Giligulgul, Wonglepong.*

*Iron rations come in handy
On the way to Dirranbandi;
Passengers have died of hunger
During halts at Garradung(-er).*

*Let us toast, before we part,
Those who travel, stout of heart,
Drunk or sober, rain or shine,
On a Queensland railway line.*

From the Queensland Centenary
Songbook

The Sa

CHAPTER 7

NARROW GAUGE 1943 *to* 1971

MR MILL'S MOUNTAINS AN 'S' OF THE WEST

Double-heading S class 4-8-2s crossing the wooden trestle at Balingup in January, 1966. No. 548, Gardener is in charge of the Bunbury-bound goods, assisted by no. 550, Hardie.

Adrian Gunzburg

Australia, 1942: Air attacks on Darwin and the north-west coast. Midget submarines penetrate Sydney Harbour; off the coast, mines and torpedoes send ships to the bottom. In New Guinea and across the islands of the south-west Pacific, the Japanese army makes a relentless southward advance.

Against this desperate backdrop of a nation faced with the threat of invasion, Australia's railways were in crisis, groaning under the weight of moving men and supplies towards the northern frontiers.

In Melbourne early in 1942, the recently formed Commonwealth Land Transport Board (CLTB) met to consider an urgent agenda item – reinforcing the locomotive power of the narrow gauge States, which were bearing the brunt of forward defence.

Sir Harold Clapp who had transferred from heading the aircraft industry to 'supremo' of land transport pressed for a powerful locomotive that could work without restriction on all 3 ft 6 in lines. Time was of the essence, the nation's survival hung in the balance and Clapp wanted action now.

Out of the west came two men seconded to the CLTB to hurry the introduction of a new locomotive. One was Joseph Ellis, Commissioner of the Western Australian Government Railways, and the other Frederick Mills, his Chief Mechanical Engineer. Ellis, a civil engineer, recommended that only an articulated locomotive of the Garratt type could satisfy the national need, as Clapp had specified.[1] And he spoke with the conviction as head of the only State railway that currently operated numerous classes of Garratt locomotives.

Ellis' report nominated three types of Garratt – heavy, medium and light. While the WAGR would accept a 'medium' engine, Queensland's tight curves and light track determined that the 'light' Garratt design offered the only practical solution. Thus was born the ASG – the Australian Standard Garratt, the locomotive that was to hang like an albatross around the neck of the man who designed it.

The WAGR emblem

Author's collection

War Cabinet in August 1942 approved the building of 30 locomotives, designating the CLTB, under Ministry of Munitions direction, as the design and construction authority. At a meeting in November, Cabinet increased the order to 65 locomotives.

As the only locomotive engineer familiar with the Garratt (he was involved in the design of the Msa, built at Midland Workshops) Mills took up the appointment in Melbourne as the CLTB's design and construction engineer for the new project. In short, the ASG was 'his' locomotive.

Mills immediately found himself up against a mountain of opposition. Queensland wanted no part in operating a Garratt. The

P.L. Charrett

The 14 ASGs that operated on Tasmanian Government tracks were all out of service by 1957. In contrast, the Emu Bay Company's five ASG class, as seen above, lasted until August, 1963.

Queensland Railways Commissioner, Mr P.R. Wills urged the building of more C17 class, a well tried and trusted medium powered locomotive that could run almost anywhere on QR metals.[2] Wills condemned the proposed Garratt as simply a 'War machine,' having no useful purpose in peacetime when like any tank or gun it would be good only for scrap. Tasmania, the Garratt pioneer, also wanted to distance itself from the project in view of the order for additional Q class freight locomotives placed with the Clyde Engineering Company. Strangest of all, the Commonwealth Railways, operator of the far-flung North and Central Australia lines, showed a marked lack of interest in utilising the new locomotive.

Commissioner Wills added to the flames of dissent in claiming that a CLTB sub-committee of mechanical engineers had rejected the Garratt solution in preference for the C17. But Clapp would hear nothing of a 20-year-old QR design and countenanced no delay. Time was of the essence. American forces were beginning to pour into Australia, freight yards were clogged with war material awaiting movement, the narrow gauge railways were grappling with trainloads never before contemplated; the move to reinforce northern defences took priority over all else.

Clapp personally ram-rodded the ASG decision through the CLTB, Wills later claimed at a Royal Commission hearing. As Director-General of the Board, Clapp reported directly to the Federal Government. Clapp's decision held.[3]

Mills was given drawing office space in the former creche above the platforms of Flinders Street Station; ironically Clapp had established the creche for mothers on shopping expeditions during his innovative years as Chairman of the Victorian Railways. The team of 15 engineers and senior draftsmen drawn from various State railways – with the exception of Queensland – worked six and seven-day weeks. In winter they wore overcoats and hats to keep out the Melbourne chill; in summer they felt close to boiling point as the sun bore down on the Flinders Street dome.

Frederick Mills, Chief Mechanical Engineer of the WAGR, 1940-49.

Author's collection

Before him Mills had a blank sheet of paper, his only reference point being un-detailed outline drawing No. 120328 which Beyer, Peacock had sent to the Queensland Railways as a speculative measure a few years before.[4] For some of the detail work, he could turn to his design of the West's S class 4-8-2, which was now under construction in Midland Workshops. Otherwise, every feature and measurement of the ASG would have to be devised in the Flinders Street Station creche. More, the locomotive would have to be in steam within 12 months.

It was an ambitious project and the first of its kind to be undertaken in Australia. It would be hard to find a case where so many complications have entered into the hurried production of a locomotive. Normally when an engine is designed only one of the type is produced and it is put into traffic for perhaps several years before others are manufactured.[5]

Queensland's 8-ton axle load and tight curves restricted fixed wheelbase to 12ft 6in, and 120 tons would be the maximum allowable weight of a locomotive intended to produce a tractive effort of around

34,000lbs. Different types of couplings were used in individual States, and braking systems differed between Queensland and the others. Enlargement of boiler and firebox specifications and expanding coal and water spaces for working on the Central Australia Railway added an undesirable $9^1/_2$-tons to the design. The compensating weight removal surgery necessitated reducing frame- stay plate thickness, cutting holes in boiler frames and resorting to hollow control rods.

Late Ken Rogers / Author's collection

Author's collection

The reduction accomplished by this means is, according to engineering standards, a radical departure from orthodox design, not so much from the point of view of the methods employed or as regards a mere reduction in weight, but more importantly from the aspect of the large aggregate of reduced weight.[6]

Three hundred drawings had to be completed to juggle the supply lines from 105 separate sub-contractors, many

Top: Slogging through Albion on a north-bound freight, the ASG is portrayed in the wartime role to which it was assigned on the Queensland Railways.

Above: Built at Midland Workshops, the Msa was exceptional as the only Garratt in the Southern Hemisphere not from Beyer, Peacock or its contractors.

of them having no previous experience with the railway industry. From these foundries and machine shops, the parts had to be fed to four widely scattered assembly plants. Midland Workshops were programmed to complete 10 locomotives; Islington 12, Newport 16, Clyde Engineering 27. Ultimately three of Newport's order was cancelled while Clyde's production reduced to 22.[7]

The first ASG emerged from Newport just 12 months after design began, and four months after the start of construction.[8] Numbered G1, it was a far cry from the trim little Beyer, Peacock Garratts with which the WAGR was identified. The ASG measured 65 ft overall, and its 200 lb boiler pressure on a 4-6-2 + 2-6-4 wheel arrangement with 4 ft driving wheels produced a tractive effort of 34,251 lbs. In contrast, Queensland's C17 was a 21,000 lbs engine.

By November 1943, all three narrow gauge States – Queensland, Western Australia and Tasmania were operating the ASG. Queensland was to receive 49 locomotives (in fact they took 23, of which 10 were purchased and 13 retained on lease from the Commonwealth); Tasmania would take eight while Western Australia's number would grow to 25. One locomotive was sold directly to the Australian Portland Cement Company's railway, at Fyansford near Geelong.

Adrian Gunzburg

No. 542, Bakewell *displays the abbreviated modification to Fred Mills' distinctive boiler-top cowling, which was also a feature of his ASG design.*

Thirty locomotives had been intended for the Central Australia Railway. Yet in a continuing bizarre turn of events, the Commonwealth Government's own system, despite the modifications to fuel spaces undertaken on their behalf, blankly refused to accept the ASG. In Port Augusta, a young CME, Eric Adam had studied Mr Mills' drawings and demanded some 27 'fixes' to the design. But the submissions were ignored, and with the Commissioner's support, Adam ruled that Alice Springs would never see an ASG.

Yet railwaymen initially seemed impressed with the power and apparent free steaming capability of the new locomotives; though speed was officially limited to 45 mph (72 kph) or less on freight trains, bursts of up to 50 mph (80 kph) were reported at times when the ASG was assigned

to passenger runs. In Queensland, Garratt working was concentrated between Brisbane-Maryborough and Bundaberg-Rockhampton on the lower section of the North Coast line which had reached saturation point; double-headed freight trains and their additional crews were eliminated as a single ASG steamed out with 520-ton loads. Given the brief assistance of a bank engine over the Eumundi Range and from Monkland to Gympie, the QR's full authorised 650 tons could be taken through to Rockhampton by Mr Mill's new locomotive.

The ASG honeymoon lasted for about four months before the troubles began to erupt.

In July 1944, Mills attended a Melbourne conference of the CLTB mechanical engineers sub-committees which called for significant modifications to the ASG. Structural soundness was questioned. A particular item at issue was the designer's choice of the variable resistance form of compensated springing of the bogies, instead of the more accepted alternative of constant resistance springing. Variable resistance springing might be satisfactory for well laid tracks – Mills was said to have taken the idea from the LNER's latest Pacifics – but Australia was no England and its light and twisting narrow gauge could only lead to trouble, with the finding:

> 'The design is open to serious objection.'[9]

Three months later the CLTB summoned a special meeting in Canberra where the QR representatives were openly hostile to ASG operation, Tasmania reported problems and the Commonwealth Railways showed no sign of wanting to buy into trouble. Sudden and often undetected derailment of the flangeless leading driving wheels, awkwardness of cab controls, poor forward vision from the cab windows, and overheating in tunnels headed the list of complaints from mechanical staff and engine crews alike. Firemen disliked the side dump ashpans and spoke of exhaustion in trying to feed coal into a 35 sq ft grate which in some instances was almost twice as large as that of the narrow gauge machines on which they normally worked. Sometimes they had to wrap bags around their legs as a protection against searing heat from the low-positioned firebox door.

Recognising that most likely it had been landed with a lemon, the Commonwealth began to advertise for ASG buyers in Australia and abroad but at this stage found no takers. In view of the CR's non-participation, numbers should have been reduced. Of the authorised 65 locomotives, eight were never assembled though components manufacture continued on the grounds that 'it was cheaper to build than cancel and incur a compensation pay-out to the sub-contractors.'

The final ASG was delivered in December, 1945.Recognised as a 'fixer' Fred Shea was called to the aid of the ailing ASG. His diary records, probably at Harold Clapp's instigation, that ...

> I have been requested to personally take over from the Munitions Department the supervision of the Australian Standard Garratt Locomotive project and to prepare and execute a programme of redesign and reconstruction of these locomotives with the object of making them thoroughly satisfactory and roadworthy and acceptable to the State Railway concerned.[10]

However the former CME who had ushered in South Australia's big engines made not much impact on the Garratt, for other individual events were now in control of the locomotive's destiny. In September, 1945, exactly two years after G1 entered service, the QR ceased operating its 23 ASGs.[11] Though some in-State loyalty had been maintained, in November Mills' own enginemen in voicing vehement protests against the ASG ('unwieldy, unsafe, uneconomical') brought about a Royal Commission. Headed by Mr Justice A Wolff, of the W.A. Supreme Court, the inquiry ran from November until the following April and called witnesses in all States.

Adrian Gunzburg

Among those who appeared were the respected Chief Mechanical Engineers of other railway departments – Andrew Ahlston (VR), Harold Young (NSWGR) and Frank Harrison (SAR). Commissioner Ellis, regarded as one of Mills' few close friends, defended his CME throughout the hearing. Withstanding attacks on the ASG – the enginemen's union

One of the S class with a larger tender was no. 544, Hallowell, waiting for its train at Collie shed in 1966.

had prepared a list of 24 grievances – would have been a draining experience for the designer yet it underlined the determination and confidence, or was it bloody mindedness, of a man who believed in the correctness of his work.

'I cannot understand how such a statement could have been made,' commented Judge Wolff on earlier claims at a Melbourne meeting by

Dr. P.A Collin

WAGR management that the ASG had given satisfaction in Western Australia and that no difficulties had been experienced.[12] In this context Commissioner Ellis had obtained State Government approval to purchase the 10 Midland-built ASGs which were in service under lease from the Commonwealth; shortly afterwards he recommended the purchase of an additional 15 locomotives.

It is clear that the Chief Mechanical Engineer (Mr Mills, the designer of the locomotive) and the Chief Traffic Manager (Mr Evans) had no hesitation in supporting the recommendation. The Commonwealth at the time was asking approximately £18,000 for each locomotive and the two officials thought that by comparison with the S class locomotive, one of the newest and most powerful engines on the State system, which cost £16,000, the ASG locomotive was good

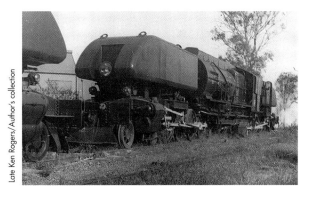

Late Ken Rogers/Author's collection

buying. Subsequently, it seems, by the use of various arguments, the purchase of the locomotives was arranged at £12,000 each.[13]

Evans and Mills sought to buy a further five but the order did not proceed, allowing the WAGR to stay with a roster of 25 ASGs, the highest number of any State. Keeping in mind that the ASGs built in the East were averaged at £25,000 each, and the final engine cost £34,000, perhaps Messrs Evans and Mills were not amiss when they recognised 'good buying'.

But the West's troubles were not over. In November 1946 the union called a strike which lasted 16 days in protest at the continued failure of the ASG. Engines which had been withdrawn for repair were 'black banned' if returned to service unmodified; soon the Government could see that a crisis point was approaching in the State's transport system. The terms of settlement, negotiated directly between Government and Union undertook the completion of the modification program. Flanges were provided

Far left: No. 549, Greenmount *has been restored to working order by dedicated volunteers of the ARHS in Western Australia. Full length cowling has been returned to the boiler top in a rebuilding effort that occupied 10 years, commencing at the Bassendean Museum premises and later transferring to Midland Junction.*

Above: Surplus ASG class in store at Rocklea sidings, Brisbane in April, 1944.

on the leading driving wheels, axle boxes and pivot centres received attention, steam blows were reduced and adjustments made to improve the reliability of the engine steam brake. Gradually the ASG returned to traffic and for up to another 12 years would serve the State usefully until the arrival of the last modern steam locomotives and the first diesel-electrics ended a chequered career.

In his evidence to the Royal Commission, Harold Young, CME of the New South Wales Government Railways said he was of the opinion that the ASG was fundamentally 'quite all right'...

> Its faults are mainly ones of detail and I feel sure that the engine could be made to run quite all right with a little more thought and a little more care on the part of those who would be entrusted with the correction of the faults. The general outline is good and basically sound and I see no reason why the engine should not give many years of useful work.[14]

The Federal Auditor-General in a report of 30 June 1946 found that the ASG project had concluded in a distinct financial loss of some £1,500,000 for the Commonwealth. Average cost of the locomotives was £25,000 apiece, yet when sold to the ultimate operators in Tasmania and South Australia, they went for around half this figure.

'Makers…1943…Midland Junction' reads the builders plate beneath S542's number at East Perth.

But how does one put a price on a nation's defence? Who can count the number of Army trains, supply trains, freights and sometimes passenger trains that these gangling black engines of the myriad dancing wheels

Brian and Jan Lillis

and whirling side-rods hauled out of Brisbane and Perth on the long drag up the North Coast and to the Eastern Goldfields? Perhaps Commissioner Wills wasn't far wrong. If the Army's tanks are made for battle and then discarded, maybe the ASG should be viewed in much the same light, for its purpose was to assist in the railways fighting a war, to keep the men and munitions moving, to contribute to the enemy's defeat.

Substantial evidence (especially after the provision of flanges on all driving wheels) argues against dismissing the

Adrian Gunzburg

Garratt as a dismal failure. With modifications, the Tasmanian Railways continued to operate their ASG (now 14 in all) until October 1957 and the Emu Bay Company which purchased six locomotives 'second hand' kept them working until August 1963.[15] In Western Australia, despite the opposition, the final ASG went in January 1957. For stop gap purposes (while new Beyer-Garratts were on order!) the South Australian Railways purchased six used ASG from the West; Fyansford's lone locomotive was only displaced by a diesel in 1957 and now resides in the North Williamstown Railway Museum.

Will it ever steam again? S547, Lindsay (right) with its boiler stripped down, stands on a siding of the Bellarine Peninsula Railway, between Queenscliff and Drysdale, Victoria.

Below: A generous plume of whitish smoke heralds a W class 4-8-2 assisting S550 Hardie as they hurry through Newlands with a south-western freight in May 1969.

Though his work was criticised yet fundamentally exonerated in Justice Wolff's 83-page report of August 1946, none of this trial and woe proved helpful to the health of Frederick Mills. Nor did searching inquiries into the management of Midland Workshops and then the whole structure of

Author's photograph

the WAGR, which followed soon after the First Royal Commission. In 1948 he went to London to discuss the specifications of the improved Pm/Pmr class, the WAGR's latest Pacific type passenger locomotive. The late Ray Minchin, who had worked in the Midland Drawing Office under 'Freddie' reported meeting his old Chief in early 1949 and noting the man's drawn and haggard look.

Mills died while dining at a Perth hotel on 22 June, 1949. He was aged 51. In its Annual Report the WAGR mourned the 'untimely end to a brilliant career'. Born at Newcastle-on-Tyne on 15 August, 1897 Mills began his railway career in an indentured apprenticeship as a fitter and turner; at R & W Hawthorn Leslie & Co he gained his first experience as a draftsman. He spent six years at Armstrong Whitworth in Scotswood, promoted to the post of Leading Locomotive Draftsman; quite probably he would have worked on the design of the big engines ordered by Commissioner Webb in 1925 for the South Australian Railways. Though evidence is lacking, it is reasonable to speculate that this association with the broad gauge power of a 'land of sunshine down under' drew him to Australia – not to the SAR, but to the narrow gauge of the West, where a job was offering.

Appointed as a Locomotive Design Draftsman, he began work at Midland Junction Workshops in April 1926 and by November, 1931 had been promoted to Chief Draftsman. It is fairly said that from this moment, the pursuit of locomotive design seriously began in the WAGR. In 1940 he replaced the retiring J.W.R. Broadfoot to become CME. Early in his Midland career, Mills took a leading role in shaping the Msa. Based on improvements to earlier Beyer, Peacock Ms class 2-6-0 + 0-6-2, this was reputedly the first Garratt built in the Southern Hemisphere. The Pr express engine, again an improvement on the original North British P class Pacifics, was another of his assignments, 10 being built at Midland in 1938–39. Mills has been described as an engineer 'with a zeal and capacity for work' who would spend long hours, if needs be, in pursuit of an objective. Lesser known design contributions attributed to him in the WAGR included the Y-form locomotive coupled wheel spokes (used on the S, Pm/Pmr and ASG) and various types of drawgear and screw couplings.

But it is through the S class that Mills should be best remembered in the West. This purposeful 4-8-2 was the first and largest locomotive truly designed and built at Midland Workshops.[16] Proposed as a major and much overdue jump forward from the Fs 4-8-0 of 1902-1913, it appeared in 1943

Terry Verney

S549 Greenmount, finished in authentic black livery, double-heading with Pm class Pacific no. 706 on a Hotham Valley excursion at Harvey in October, 1997.

as a 119-ton machine, exerting a 30,685 lbs tractive effort. Mills authored a paper on an all-welded plate frame proposed for the S class, which in 1938 won him the James Lincoln Arc Welding Foundation award of £900 in New York. 'It just shows that a Western Australian engineer has a talent equal to any in the world in the field of welding,' said the department's magazine, commenting on Mills' success.[17] (Midland employed conventional riveted frames building the S class.)

Origin of the S class belonged to a 1930s design of a quite spectacular 4-8-4 tank locomotive, with three cylinders, which would have speeded freight trains between Northam and Fremantle, and avoided disrupting Perth's suburban timetables.[18] The tank locomotive never materialised, but by the late 1930s Mills was incorporating features of the design in his new mixed traffic 4-8-2, distinguished in being the West's first Mountain class and appropriately bearing the names of Western Australian mountains.[19]

Similarity is evident in the overlapping features of the two locomotives – the S and ASG. In effect, one locomotive had been designed

Terry Verney

The line-up of active motive power at the Hotham Valley Railway's shed at Pinjarra - between a W (4-8-2) and Pr (4-6-2) stands S549, Greenmount.

and built when the priority for another overtook it. Both were engines without any visible funnel, this being sunk into the 'streamlined' combing that ran along the boiler crest, which also housed the pipe and valve connections to Mills' choice of a front end regulator. Gone, too, was the traditional dome, the designer's preference being for an internal perforated collector pipe. The leading and third driving wheels were flangeless and an exhaust steam injector was located on the fireman's side.[20] Generous inlet and exhaust passages cast integral with the steam chest covers accounted for the particularly 'bulbous' ends at the cylinder area.

As WAGR engines were ever destined to cope with the poor thermal qualities of Collie's sub-bituminous coal, a grate area of 40 sq ft was regarded as none too large for the power required from the new Mountain class, with its 200 psi boiler. Three locomotives appeared in 1943, beginning in February just six months before the delivery of Midland's first ASG. The Garratt program and various wartime material shortages delayed production of the next two engines until 1945 with the delivery of the final seven extending through to 1947.[21]

Fred's critics, which he did not lack, claimed that he tended to rush design innovations without permitting sufficient time for testing. It is noted that in the S class he adopted Cartazzi type suspension in place of equalised (or compensated) springing of the rear trucks. As illustrated in the Royal Commission, he also avoided compensated springing on the ASG, despite the flangeless leading driving wheels which were the cause of so much trouble; also favoured were the Cyclone spark arrestor and servo-piston

Bryan and Jan Lillis

The Mills Y-spoked driving wheels no longer turn on S542 Bakewell *standing at East Perth terminal.*

regulator valves, common to both the Mountain and the Garratt designs.

Mills' new locomotive, of course, drew the obligatory objections from the enginemen's union, but the problems were overcome; much of these protests appeared to be related to the antiquated fear of big engines putting men out of a job. After 'teething troubles', the S proved to be a dependable mixed traffic machine[22] hauling wheat to the port, coal from Collie, and sometimes rostered on passenger duties, though dramatic bursts of speed were hardly likely given 4 ft diameter driving wheels. The 'Sammies' as the S class was sometimes known lasted until the very end of regular steam on the WAGR; no. 548 was the last to run on Christmas eve, 1971. Three survivors are still to be found– one is on static display at East Perth terminal (542 – *Bakewell*) another belongs to the Bellarine Peninsula Railway in Victoria (547 – *Lindsay*) while a third (549 – *Greenmount*) is back in steam, operated for the Australian Railway Historical Society.

Fred Mills was of a controversial character. He was undoubtedly a clever engineer, but poor at communicating and listening, and making few close friends. 'Freddie' as they called him was regarded by his subordinates in the Mechanical Branch as quite a martinet – and a waxed moustache rather supported this image. Much feared was his regular Friday afternoon appearance – when at 3 o'clock, with pipe in hand, he began an inspection of the drawing boards, his finely-tuned memory knowing precisely at which point the draftsman had reached on his previous weekly visit.

Because of his strong personality and perceived authoritarian air, Ray Minchin concluded that 'some people were out to get Freddie' which did not assist his health and equilibrium in the wake of the ASG trauma.[23] Yet, his reputation as an able administrator saw him appointed Acting Commissioner in 1947. He was probably the most academically inclined of Australia's locomotive designers, given of a precise, clear and practical mind that tended to suffer fools none too gladly. He lectured in 1939 at the University of Western Australia to under-graduates in the School of Mechanical Engineering. He employed experimental stress analysis in developing his Y-form spokes for locomotive wheels. In the making of the ASG, he bore much of the design work himself, unfortunately having little time to listen to criticisms which could have avoided certain of the problems that subsequently marred the locomotive's performance. But at the time he was obviously Australia's only locomotive engineer experienced in Garratt design.

Bryan and Jan Lillis

He was an active member of the Institution of Engineers, Australia and the British-based Institution of Locomotive Engineers and published papers in the professional journals. At his initiative, the British Institution formed its first group of Australian members. He led a private life, apart from membership of the Royal Perth Yacht Club, which he had joined in 1927, shortly after arriving from England. He and his wife, Alice, whom he wed in 1929 were without children. Their married life began at Mt Lawley, then they moved to North Perth and finally to Adelaide Terrace.

Maybe it took a controversial character to be the author of the fastest and most urgent locomotive production program Australia has ever attempted — one that inevitably came together in wartime, 'warts and all'. Perhaps it is better to view Fred Mills in his contribution of the S class to the ranks of Steam's Last Giants.

Outside East Perth terminal, S542 Bakewell *rests in the care of the ARHS, WA Division.*

Ghost Garratts

The end of the line – that was my home town.
My first after-dark remembrance was of rattle-rushing rails
And a huge keening lament, grieving the night down.
I built my own language – those belling wails
Were "oo-ers"; the bustling expulsion of smoke and steam,
"Funk comin out've 'funket." Memory: a team,
My grandpop and me, hand in hand at the goodsyard gate.
Fear and wonder that men could shape this thing;
This black-barging monster which the years came to designate
My childhood's metaphor. Here was the last fling
Of the AS Garratt – a track-jumper, fireman-sweater,
Loud angry failure, in exile, a dead letter.
Dreams, reputations, shunted there to that quiet siding,
A haunt of ghost-garratts, down the line riding.

Funk - a 3 year-old's attempt to pronounce smoke.
Funket - the place where smoke emanated from –
the smoke stack.

By P.R. Hay, ARHS *Bulletin,*
June 1986.

Firs

NARROW GAUGE 1923 *to* 1964

COST-PLUS IN TASMANIA
THE Q CLASS

As a small boy in Melbourne, I can still recall my family's outrage at the sheer audacity of the Tasmanian Railways in copying the *Spirit of Progress*.

'Who do these people think they are?' exploded my cousin Lloyd upon gazing at a newspaper picture of a rather tinnily clad R class Pacific. 'Don't they know the *Spirit* belongs to Victoria?' he yelled. 'Mister Clapp should sue them for – ' His words trailed off.

Over-priced and overdue? Q16, one of the four 'cost plus' engines delivered from Clyde in 1943, stands in Launceston yards after final assembly at the nearby TGR workshops.

Andrew Dix collection

The affront was just too dreadful to articulate. Sitting around our Hornby train layout, we agreed sort of pityingly that they were just a little narrow gauge outfit so what could you expect? Our splendid S class which hauled the *Spirit* could touch seventy miles an hour. Their cloned streamliner with just a couple of carriages in tow would be lucky to reach half that speed.

Yes, small they might be, but one grows older to appreciate what a surprising mark the railways of the island State have made on Australia's locomotive history. To be sure, they were first of a class.

On the mountainous west coast in 1909 they introduced the world's first Garratt locomotives, the midget yet compound cylinder K class, an 0-4-0 + 0-4-0, the articulated brain child of English engineer Herbert Garratt who, among other things, was a consultant to the New South Wales Government Railways.[1]

The success of the K in climbing 1-in-25 grades and rounding 99ft radius curves on the spectacular 2ft gauge North East Dundas Tramway inspired the Tasmanians three years later to invest in two of the world's first passenger Garratts for the Hobart to Launceston express on the 3ft 6in main line.

Late C.C. Singleton/Author's collection

Unique, also, as the only eight-cylinder Garratts ever built, their high-wheel M class could touch 55 mph (88 kph) though their record was somewhat suspect after the unfortunate Campania derailment of 1916 in which four were killed. Simultaneously imported from Manchester came the twin L class 2-6-0 + 0-6-2 Beyer Garratts that at the time were Australia's most powerful freight engines. After being put aside in the 1930's, they were reconditioned in 1943 and lasted for a few more years.

Back at the 2ft gauge, the railways had purchased in 1900 an unusual 2-6-4 'divided drive' articulated tank locomotive from Hagans, of Erfurt in Germany. Known as the J class, it worked the North East Dundas tram none too successfully because of an excessive weight of 41 tons; failure of the mines closed the line in 1930. Not far distant, the Mount Lyell Mining and Railway Company ran 0-4-2 Abt system tank locomotives on one of Australia's only two rack lines, climbing the 1-in-16 grade of Sailor Jack's

This 4-4-0 Ab class suggested the sort of locomotive one would find on Tasmanian lines in the old days – small, colonial and Beyer, Peacock.

Divide between Regatta Point and the Queenstown mines. (This spectacular track is being restored as a tourist railway.)

In 1929, Tasmania's major private railway operated by the Emu Bay Company from Burnie to Rosebery and Zeehan caught the attention of locomotive engineers with the introduction of three world heavyweight class Beyer - Garratts for ore haulage between Rosebery and Burnie across the 1-in-33 of wild west coast terrain. These 4-8-2 + 2-8-4 machines, weighing 132 tons and exerting 37,610 lbs tractive effort stood among the most powerful Garratts built by Beyer, Peacock until after World War 2.

Tasmania's railway system began in 1871 with the 5 ft 3in gauge Launceston and Western Company. However their broad gauge ambitions proved too costly and in 1888 a rapid conversion occurred after the Tasmanian Main Line Company built to the cheaper colonial gauge between Hobart and Launceston. By 1890 the Government had taken over the private systems; generally speaking (with the exception of the Garratt) locomotive policy settled into 19th century style four-and six-coupled engines, neat and sprightly but hardly among steam's giants.

An enforced and major rehabilitation program of the 1920s, under the leadership of Commissioner George Smith rather changed the mainland's perspective from 'Tassie's Toy Trains' to one of somewhat incredulous respect. Heavier rails and improved operating facilities and practices enabled Tasmania to introduce Australia's first Mountain type locomotives which among the government narrow gauge systems back in

1922 were by far the most powerful. The 27,200 lbs tractive effort exerted by the new 105-ton Q class contrasted with the ratings of the biggest 4-8-0 style freight engines elsewhere: Queensland's C19, 23,500 lbs, the West's Fs, 23,268 lbs and South Australia's T, 21,903.[2]

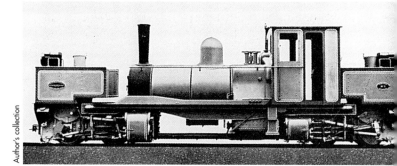

In a switch from Tasmania's traditional Beyer, Peacock connection, the two men responsible for the Q design, Deeble and Leslie turned to a mixture of American and British practice in setting the specifications for the husky new 4-8-2. Further, manufacture would be at an Australian workshop, not in Manchester.

L.C. Leslie had been Chief Draftsman and Acting Chief Mechanical Engineer of the Commonwealth Railways during construction of the east-west line. After returning from service in the AIF, he entered 'private practice' in Melbourne which is where he was commissioned by W. R. Deeble, Chief Mechanical Engineer of the Tasmanian Government Railways (TGR) to collaborate as consulting engineer in the design of a new locomotive.

Tasmania's plan to acquire modern motive power began immediately after World War 1 when proposals were sought from a number of established builders including Armstrong Whitworth, Kitson, North British,

P.L. Charrett

Baldwin and Montreal Locomotive Works (MLW). On the home front, Thompsons of Castlemaine were among those who made a response. Existing narrow gauge designs, such as Queensland's C17 and even the Emu Bay Company's 4-8-0, produced by Dubs in 1897 were checked for suitability.

Currency exchange rates prohibited overseas dealings and with Australian companies eager to obtain work, after the calling of tenders, an order was placed with Perry Engineering, of South Australia, whereupon Thompsons immediately cried 'foul!' However the resulting Royal Commission of 1920 exonerated the TGR management from allegations that the Victorian builder had been unfairly treated; in fact the contract with Perry was found to be quite properly awarded.

Perhaps one reason for suspicion on behalf of Thompsons was the emergence of the somewhat controversial figure of Henry Teesdale Smith as a go-between in securing the order for South Australia. Teesdale Smith, now resident in Adelaide, had been a prominent contractor responsible for railway and tramway construction in New South Wales, South Australia,

Left: Tasmania's K1, one of two of the world's first Garratts, built for the North East Dundas Tramway on the West Coast in 1909.

Above: On the Emu Bay Railway the ASG won a new lease of life; purchased mostly from the Queensland Railways they were rostered for passenger and freight trains on the scenic West Coast line from Burnie.

Tasmania, Western Australia, and for portion of the Trans-Australian line. His involvement almost inevitably led to accusations of what might be called 'slick business dealings'. In union ranks he was known as 'Little Napoleon' and the *Westralian Worker* labelled him 'a cute customer of the eel family who will want a lot of watching'.

Perry Engineering's approach to the design of the required 10 locomotives is understood to have been based on an outline drawing of a 4-6-2 submitted by MLW. However William Rufus Deeble, now in his 64th year and nearing retirement after some 40 years with Tasmania's railways, appears to have been intent on leaving his mark on the shaping of the State's new locomotive policy. At his recommendation, six locomotives designated Q class, would be introduced as the 4-8-2 Mountain type, while the remaining four locomotives, known as R class, would be 4-6-2 Pacifics. The Q class were to work principally on the southern portion, of the Hobart – Launceston main line, yet also be available for heavy traffic on the Fingal, Western and Derwent Valley routes, while the R class would be dedicated to main line passenger operation.

The contributions of British and American practice were evident in the choice of plate frames, while adopting the wide U.S.style firebox. Commonality figured prominently in Deeble and Leslie's approach, covering such major items as cab, firebox, tenders, bogies and pony trucks; the boiler barrel of the Mountain type was obviously made longer than that of the Pacific. The purpose of the locomotives gave the Q a 48-inch wheel (R class diameter was 55 inches) with the leading driver unflanged; axle load remained within $12^1/_2$ tons.

After delays awaiting the arrival of materials ordered from Britain (boiler plate, superheater tubes, wheels), construction of the Q progressed through1921 at Perry's two plants – the boiler work at Gawler and frames and assembly in Adelaide. Q1 was completed and tested in June 1922, and after dismantling for shipment and re-erection at Launceston Workshops in July, the big black machine entered service late in August.[3] Q6, the last of the Mountain class batch, reached Launceston with Pacific R1 in March 1923. The four trim R class effectively wheeled their passenger trains across the 1-in-40 main line grades and achieved their own claim to fame as the first wide firebox Pacific type on an Australian government system. Two class members, nos. 3 and 4 were the villains which aroused our boyhood ire when they appeared in *Spirit of Progress* styling in 1937 at the head of the

Below: The historical connection between Herbert Garratt's design and Tasmanian railways was further emphasised in 1938 when the Emu Bay Company imported three 4-8-2+2-8-4 Beyer-Garratts which rated among the world's heaviest built for the narrow gauge.

Below Right: Tasmania's 1912 M class was the first and only eight-cylinder Garratt. The 'double Atlantic' was capable of maintaining an express schedule on the Hobart-Launceston line.

regular Day and Boat expresses.[4]

Deeble, who had begun his railway career at the Phoenix Foundry, Ballarat in 1879, and then joined the Tasmanian Main Line Company, concluded his almost 45 years with the locomotive in 1923, just long enough to witness his impressive Mountain and Pacifics begin a new motive power era on the TGR. The Q class rewrote the train load diagrams and though much larger than their predecessors, proved popular with crews; in the words of Tasmanian rail historian Andrew Dix, 'they were the pride of the TGR.' L.C. Leslie subsequently joined Perry and became

P.L. Charrett

Author's collection

the company's Chief Engineer from 1924. Though the Adelaide builder opted out of the heavy locomotive business, his name is associated with the stable of 2ft gauge cane tramway locomotives that bore the name 'Perry' prominently on their smokebox door.

The success of the powerful Q class (even the broad gauge Victorians were overshadowed) won approval for a further three locomotives to be built at Walkers Limited, of Queensland – Perry having indicated their withdrawal from the heavy market. Then in 1936 came a contract for six additional Q class placed with the only bidder, Clyde Engineering, of New South Wales, at its Granville plant.

Modifications made in 1940 to a second batch of four locomotives increased boiler pressure on three (Q16, 17, 19) from 160 to 180 lbs psi,

Author's collection

The two L class of 1912 were early examples of a Beyer-Garratt freight locomotive; a motive power shortage during the second World War returned them to service.

lifting tractive effort to 30,600 lbs; later, possibly in the interests of uniformity, all boiler pressures were set at 160lb. Roller bearings and firebox thermic syphons were also included in the design handed to Clyde; unchanged from the earlier Perry and Walkers versions went the 4 ft driving wheels, 32 sq ft grate, superheating, Walschaert valve gear and tender capacity for six tons of coal and 3500 gallons of water. Axle load was $12^1/_2$ tons.

Clyde contracted to complete the Q class at a price of £18, 690 per engine, fob Launceston, with delivery in 1941 – two in May and the second pair in September. But the schedule had been devised before the outbreak of the second World War reached across the oceans, disrupting the flow of metals and machinery – much less before 7 December, 1941 when the Japanese surprise attack on Pearl Harbour brought the conflict to Australia's front door.

With absolute priority given to munitions production, which included the building of an Australian Standard Garratt locomotive, construction of the Q class immediately began to falter.[5] Tasmania

H.J.W. Stokes

Smokebox cleaning and coaling for Q4 at Hobart in December, 1960. No. 4 belonged to the original Perry contract.

admittedly was far removed from the battle zone, but the increase in wartime traffic soon had its impact on the railways. The veteran L class Beyer-Garratts were refurbished, and the need for a full complement of Q class, mainstay of heavy freight haulage spurred the Government into action. In March, 1943 the Minister for Munitions received a letter from the Premier urgently requesting completion of the Q class contract.

PDSRM Archives

Perry Engineering, of South Australia, built the first six Q class in 1923, and in parallel produced four R class passenger engines, the first 4-6-2 type in Australia to have the true 'wide firebox' Pacific design. Perry's official works photograph shows Q1 after completion at their Mile End plant.

The Premier's intervention resulted in the State railways being granted access to materials, but in a bizarre 'catch 22' situation, priority did not extend to construction, meaning that Clyde's work on the ASG continued to hold precedence. To add a little salt to the wound, enginemen from Queensland, a State without Garratt experience were sent south to Launceston to gain footplate experience on the old L class.

A letter from Granville head office contained the final straw: unless Tasmania agreed to switch to a cost-plus contract as with Clyde's other defence orders, no delivery date could be fixed. The State Transport Commission with much reluctance accepted the revised contract, but it was a waste of ink. Perhaps the Federal Government, with its eyes fixed to the

Author's collection

Cost-plus in Tasmania

northern frontiers did not take Tasmania's supplications seriously. Perhaps they believed Fred Mills, designer of the ASG who told the Commonwealth Land Transport Board that Tasmania was prepared to await their ASG allocation (the first of eight Garratts arrived in April, 1944) and the Q deliveries could be set aside[6]; it was a statement hotly contested by the Transport Commission.

To put an end to frustration, the Transport Commission directed the railways General Manager to plan for completion of the Q class in Launceston Workshops, a facility that had no background in building big locomotives; but these were extraordinary times. The first two locomotives of the final order were shipped from Sydney in November, 1943 with the understanding that eight NSWGR fitters from Eveleigh would be assigned to Clyde for the completion of the two remaining. Again Tasmania missed out! On arrival at Granville, the men were redirected under Munitions orders to work on the ASG.

The last two Q class, numbers 18 and 19, were delivered unfinished in March and December, 1944 for assembly in Launceston Workshops. Clyde claimed £32,000 for each of the Tasmanian engines which, when combined with costs incurred in Launceston raised the price per locomotive to somewhere in the order of £36,000 – close on 100% above the original contract figures. Tasmania's Q class program concluded with the setting of two records – the introduction of Australia's first Mountain type and, on a pound-for-pound basis, contributing one of the most expensive locomotives ever completed among steam's smaller last giants.

Note: The Tasmanian Railways continued their record-making in 1950 with the imported X class, Australia's first mainline diesel-electrics. These locomotives, and the Launceston-built Y class that followed led to the withdrawal of the last of the gallant Q class in 1964, except for No 5 retained in the Transport Museum, Glenorchy for exhibition.[7]

Previous page: A northbound freight leaving Hobart behind Q11, first of the Clyde-built locomotives secured under a 1936 contract which stretched until 1943 before the final of the 10 locomotives was delivered.

Above: No mistaking the similarity between the streamlining of Tasmania's express R class no.4 and its broad gauge (above left) 'big brother', the Victorian Railways' S class of Spirit of Progress *fame. Some Melbournites murmured that he TGR had committed loco-plagiarism.*

THE SPIRITUAL RAILWAY

The line to Heaven by Christ was made,
With heavenly truth the Rails are laid,
From Earth to Heaven the Line extends,
To Life Eternal where it ends.

Repentance in the Station then,
Where Passengers are taken in,
No fee for them is there to pay,
For Jesus is Himself the way.

God's Word is the First Engineer,
It points the way to Heaven so clear,
Through Tunnels dark and dreary here,
It does the way to Glory steer.

God's Love the Fire, his Truth the Steam,
Which drives the Engine and the Train,
All you who would to Glory ride,
Must come to Christ in Him abide.

In First and Second and Third Class,
Repentance, Faith and Holiness.
You must the way to Glory gain,
Or you with Christ will not remain.

Come then poor Sinners, now's the time,
At any station on the Line,
If you'll repent and turn from sin,
The Train will stop and take you in.

Memorial in Ely Cathedral to a
Driver and Fireman killed in a
railway accident,
24 December, 1845.

Author's collection

The powerful lines of the Q class are evident as bursting safety valves suggest that the freight is ready to depart. When introduced in 1923, as Australia's first Mountain type, the Q's tractive effort registered it also as the country's most powerful locomotive of the narrow gauge State systems.

The hierarchy of the NSWGR assemble around 3806, first of the new Pacific type built at Eveleigh in 1943. Commissioner Tom Hartigan is fifth from the left, next to him (holding his hat) is the CME, Harold Young. To the Commissioner's left is Bill Armstrong, who will become CME upon Harold Young's retirement in 1950. No. 3806 was the first of the non-streamlined C38 class.

CHAPTER 9

LAST OF THE PACIFICS

C38 OF NEW SOUTH WALES

Standard Gauge 1943 to 1970

QUEENSLAND'S BB18¼

Narrow Gauge 1951 to 1970

SRA/ Author's collection

vivors

For those who remember, or like to read about remembering, 1943 was a vintage year for the locomotive watcher. In retrospect, in the midst of a desperate war close by Australia's front door, it might seem bizarre that this was the opportunity taken to unveil two of the country's most able and famous express power machines.

SRA/ Author's collection

Left: Approaching the completion stage, 3806 is lowered to its wheels in the Eveleigh erecting shop. The same workshops now house the surviving class members, 3801 and 3830, and the mainly volunteer teams that take care of maintenance. Thirteen of the C38 class were built in the NSWGR workshops at Eveleigh and 12 at Cardiff, near Newcastle.

Not that railway managements planned to complete them as a handy distraction from the enemy advance. Locomotives take time to design, sometimes even longer to build. Both the C38 and the 520 had been on the drawing board, in fact, before Hitler began jack-booting across Europe or Japan attacked Pearl Harbour.

As we have seen (Chapter 4) Harold Young, thwarted in his attempt to introduce an Algerian-style express Garratt,[1] turned his attention to a

SRA/ Author's collection

A Commissioner's party visits Clyde Engineering at Granville to examine 3801, first engine in the costly and late running C38 contract. All five C38 from Clyde were streamlined.

conventional fixed frame locomotive with the Pacific wheel arrangement which allowed a wide firebox. His decision was quite a change for New South Wales where for the past 50 years passenger engines had been of the 4-6-0 type with narrow fireboxes tucked between the frames.[2]

After his return from an overseas tour, Harold Young wrote a paper in 1937 which surveyed the development of the world's very fast trains and the locomotives that hauled them…

High speed trains have stimulated locomotive steam engineers to explore the possibilities of steam locomotives, and the greater attention given to the balancing of the reciprocating and revolving weights of the locomotive, together with an improvement in steam distribution in the cylinders, the use of larger boilers and wheels. The need for greater carrying capacity trains (than provided by light weight diesel trains) has led to the design and construction of super speed steam locomotives, such as the *Silver Jubilee*, 4-6-2 of the London and North Eastern Railway; *Hiawatha*, 4-4-2 of the Chicago Milwaukee St. Paul and Pacific Railroad; *Mercury*, 4-6-4 of the New York Central Railroad; and the streamlined 4-6-4 locomotive of the German Railways.[3]

In 1938 the CME began to bring to fruition his plans for locomotive design. More than 100 engineers, draftsmen and assistants were assigned at Eveleigh to advance the C38

Climbing Cowan Bank, 3817 with a Sydney-bound Newcastle Flyer air-conditioned set.

SRA/ARHS Archives

project. Young concentrated much of his emphasis on 'balancing' the locomotive and, in conformity with the Cole formula developed in the United States, achieving maximum efficiency in the boiler-cylinder relationship. All these features he described in much detail in a paper read before the Institution of Engineers in Sydney on 15 March 1944.[4]

Because of track limitations, Young's design held to the 5ft 9in diameter driving wheel that had been introduced on the C34 class back in 1909 and subsequently adopted for the C35 and C36 ten-wheelers. Obvious improvements, however, were his use of Box-pok driving wheels, roller bearings and precision powered valve gear. As with the D57, his earlier 4-8-2 (and later with the AD60), Young utilised a one-piece cast steel frame imported from America, but this time including cylinders and smokebox saddle integral with the bed.

The C38 era has arrived at Eveleigh Loco Sheds in this power parade of NSWGR express locomotives, reaching back from 1943 to the C32 class of the 1890s.

NSWGR/Dale Budd collection

David Jackson

Powerhouse Museum's 3830 fresh from an extensive rebuild at Eveleigh, takes charge of the Cockatoo Run tourist service operated by 3801 Limited on the scenic route between the South Coast and the Southern Highlands.

His most notable design advance, however, would be in the making of the splendid nickel steel boiler, which generated steam at 245lbs psi – by far the highest on an Australian railway. Five arch tubes were fitted to the large firebox.

With the outbreak of war in 1939 the availability of materials and equipment began to tighten. Consequently, class leader 3801 did not enter service until 22 January 1943. Clyde Engineering built the first five of the 200-ton locomotives to a streamlined outline, while the remaining twenty-five, in non-streamlined form, came from the Government workshops – thirteen from Eveleigh and twelve from Cardiff.

For the CME, doing business with Clyde, apart from the frustration of waiting more than four years for the delivery of the first locomotive, became a mixed bag. The Granville company had energetically lobbied the government over its lack of orders since the last D57 of 1930,[5] consequently it seems the C38 contract was issued without the normal

Sir Robert Cotton

Eveleigh Workshops is the backdrop to 3801, first engine in the thirty-strong C38 class. Operated by 3801 Limited, this first streamlined C38 is a familiar visitor on special excursion trains out of Sydney.

calling of tenders. Clyde's 1938 figures for the five engines stood at £99,225. Six years later it had risen to £215,046. The company cited changes to the C38 design and weight and wartime pressures as reasons for the substantial increase – to which could be joined the impact of a switch to the 'cost-plus formula' - shades of the Tasmanian Q class! References to the bullet-nosed shape of 3801 and its four Clyde companions would henceforth bring a grim smile to members of Young's mechanical branch and others in the railway hierarchy.

Dubbed the 'Grey Nurse' because of a drab workshop paint scheme, 3801 ran the Melbourne Express for the first time on 27 February 1943. With deliveries completed by 1949, this highly successful locomotive had supplanted the C36 on Melbourne trains, as well as running the *Newcastle Flyer* and the various Daylight air-conditioned expresses that were introduced post-war for country destinations.

The C38 grate, at 47 square feet (4.36 square metres) was more than

50 per cent larger than the C36. This fact was not lost on footplate crews on the Main South when the new locomotives entered service.[6] The use of mechanical stokers (as on the D57) had been considered but not adopted. At the bottom line, the fireman was key to performance.

With a Melbourne Express of some 460 tons, the time allowed for the C38 in climbing the 1-in-75 ruling grade between Picton and Mittagong was 58 to 62 minutes, equivalent to an average speed of just under 30 miles per hour (48 kph).[7] To sustain an engine output of 1600 IHP throughout this distance, the man in blue overalls would feed some two tons of coal to the hungry grate, equivalent to seven throws with the scoop for each minute he balanced himself on the swaying footplate.

In his memorable article 'The Grey Nurse – Thrills on a Railroad Flyer', Tom Hickey captured the subtle drama of the night that 3801 took out the Melbourne Express…

> The evening traffic at one of the Empire's greatest railway terminals is beginning to ease; passenger loadings on the local and through electrics are past the peak; soon the steel highways will be clear for the interstate and country expresses.
>
> 'It's time you whistled out, George', the Locomotive Dispatch Officer says, and a man in blue overalls climbs up into the cab of an engine on No. 15 road – an engine with no visible funnel.
>
> The clock at Sydney Station gives the time as 7.40 p.m. There is a hissing of steam as George opens the throttle of his new flier and, as she moves majestically from the steam shed, mechanics and cleaners pause in their work to glance admiringly at her huge yet shapely bulk.
>
> She is the triumph of the Chief Mechanical Engineer's Department of the New South Wales Government Railways, known to the running staffs as the 'Grey Nurse' because of her wartime colouring.
>
> Tonight she is making her maiden run with a full load on the Melbourne Express; and George, her driver, is Superintendent of Locomotive Running. He rose to that post from the steam sheds, and has driven on every road in New South Wales. But the engine he drives tonight is different. She is seventy-six feet long; the boiler pressure is the highest ever used in Australian locomotive practice.
>
> All the axles run on roller bearings with grease lubrication, and the wheel arrangement is classified as 4-6-2, a design pioneered by a New Zealand engineer; hence the name, Pacific.

SRA/ARHS Resource Centre

Author's collection

As the monster is coupled on to her train the clock shows the time as 7.46 p.m. – nine minutes to starting time. A head shunter looking up at the high footplate asks in the free-and-easy way of railwaymen, regardless of relative rank, 'Where's the other engine? I thought you had two for this load'.

George shakes his head. 'She's taking it on her own', he says, while the other shrugs his shoulders as though washing his hands of such folly, for the train standing there represents a gross load of 552 tons, while the Grey Nurse tips the scales at just on 200 tons.

At the platform extremity a signal changes from red to green – the starting signal. The clock shows 7.54 p.m. – one minute to go. A group of executives who have gathered at the engine hold a last-minute consultation with George; then far down the platform a green light is held shoulder high by the guard on the

Above: Emerging from The Gib tunnel with a Riverina Daylight, 3817 belongs to an era in the late 1940s and 1950s when Australia's highest pressure steam locomotive typified modern express train travel on the rails of New South Wales

Left: 'Gee, dad, what big wheels!' When you're small, things can seem so gi-normous, and for this young man at Eveleigh's Open Day, 3830 is no exception..

Visiting 3820 at full steam beside Victorian R class during a rare parallel run on the North East line in Victoria.

dot of time. The rich chime whistle calls. There is a hush of excitement in the group. The test is beginning.

Her exhaust deepens, the speed increases as, throbbing with power, the engine gets hold of her load with a boiler pressure of two hundred and

Proud day at Cardiff: CME Harold Young presents Commissioner Tom Hartigan with a photo of the first C38 built at the workshops.

forty-five pounds to the square inch. Her exhaust is a loud roar, but it seems to hush a little as she sweeps past old Redfern Station, as though she dipped her flag in memory of the first railway engine in the State, weighing a modest twenty-two tons, which was assembled in a paddock over there, many years ago.

Then the throttle opens again, while its music beats like a roll of drums under the overhead bridges and fly-overs till she is clear of the yards and away. The whole of the road is hers tonight – four hundred miles of starlit gleaming track over levels, up grades, and down swinging hills, over rivers and ranges, all the way to Albury...

In 1970, class leader 3801 became the first Australian steam locomotive to cross the Continent from east to west. Hauling the special excursion train *Western Endeavour*, 3801 covered a total distance of 4922 miles (7921km) on the historic journey between Sydney, Perth and return.

Many a story is told of fast runs behind the C38. The rapid-fire exhaust, the cry of a mellow chime whistle, the blur of spinning siderods together carried the message of modern express train travel along the main lines of post-war New South Wales.

The delivery of the first standard gauge *Spirit of Progress* to reach Sydney in April 1962 is one run which remains engraved on many a memory. Awaiting the headlong flight of 3830 and 3813 which took the *Spirit* north from Albury, crowds gathered to watch the historic entry of the long blue streamliner – with speeds reputed to have touched in excess of 80mph (128 kph).

Seasoned engineman Dave Thurlow recalls the epic journey – he was a fireman aboard 3830 on a final leg from Goulburn. Dave was also fireman on 3801's attempt in 1964 to set a new 'beating the two-hour mark' record between Sydney and Newcastle…

Sid Kemp and I, having been chosen to run the loco for the big occasion, discussed how we would handle the 38 to get the best out of it. The target was to beat a 36 class record run of 2 hours 10 minutes; specifically, to cover the 104 miles to Newcastle in under two hours.[8]

Our plan was to handle 3801 like a racing car in that Sid would 'give her the gun' on the straights, brake heavily prior to the curves, then power through them. On the rising grades the engine would be worked as hard as the boiler condition allowed without jeopardising water. Sid Kemp's reputation was that of a driver not afraid to 'let her go', and myself a young Eveleigh fireman full of energy and enthusiasm. We felt we had a good chance of bettering the 36 class record made with a Newcastle express back in 1938.

CME Harold Young and Commissioner F.C. Garside stand beside 3806 at the launching of Eveleigh's first C38 class.

The Superintendent of Locomotive Running, Mr Jack Carmichael would travel with us as Locomotive Inspector. Sid and I had never met Mr Carmichael in person, so the atmosphere on the footplate was rather reserved at the start. We left Central with all the fanfare and usual noisy way that only a 38 knows how! Having raised 3801 to a fine gallop with all going well I was instructed to put the second injector on around Lewisham. I asked myself 'why?' However, it's not the fireman's job to over-rule the Superintendent.

Last of the Pacifics

Somewhere around Burwood I switched the second injector off. Now comes Sid's turn; he receives a tap on the shoulder and a finger points to the brake valve. In other words 'get hold of her'. Through Strathfield, a sharp right through the points and 'into her' again. The Superintendent suddenly realises we are operating only one injector. On with the second injector! We hit the Ryde bank in fine style, but far too much water is in the boiler with the result of a very nasty 'prime'. Off go both injectors and both blow-down cocks are opened to reduce the water level as quickly as possible. But the damage has been done, valves and pistons have lost lubrication and we are working hard on a steeply rising grade. (After a 'prime', steam locomotives become very sluggish as the lubrication has been washed off the valves and pistons and with an automatic lubricator, as fitted to the 38, it is a matter of waiting for the oil to work through again).

The morale on the footplate was at low ebb but somehow we were now no longer Superintendent, Driver and Fireman but a three-man team out to right the wrong. After being behind time at Hornsby everything rushes in fine style through the dips across to Cowan. Down the Hawkesbury bank and we are back on the timetable but the objective is to get ahead of it. Jack now takes the left hand seat, and is obviously enjoying his every moment – to get his hand on the throttle is a rare opportunity for the office-bound Superintendent.

As we pass certain points, the finger goes up to let us know: two fingers, two minutes ahead of it. I only glance up from the heat of the firehole door and acknowledge. Very little talk. We are all intent on the task and there is much noise from the engine. Sid takes over again around Wyong, and there's rising excitement as the fingers keep telling of racing miles and minutes.

All goes well until we reach the station bridge at Broadmeadow – only to have a pigeon smash the driver's window and a slither of glass enters the side of Sid's head near the temple (no safety glass in those days). Jack jumps into the driver's seat, and I grab a sweat rag to apply pressure to stop the bleeding as Sid staggers to the Fireman's side. Now we're being blocked by signals, and down to a dribble at Hamilton… and so on to Newcastle where we arrive ahead of the original 36 class table – but not under the magic two hours.

Harold Young maybe has the final say. Some years later when a Sydney newspaper suggested other men had been responsible for designing the C38, he came out of retirement with all the vigour of an old Scots warrior to retaliate'. That statement is false', he said in a letter published in the *Sun-Herald* of 20 September 1970...

> I was the designer of this sophisticated locomotive and it contains many features hitherto unconventional and not practised in other Australian railways. None of my officers had experience in a design of this magnitude; indeed, all of them served their apprenticeships in the NSW Railway Workshops and were educated at Sydney Technical College. University graduates were useless for design work. All data sheets, locomotive proportions, distribution of weight on axles, method of balancing revolving weights, valve gear, kinematics diagrams, boiler proportions were prepared by me for the guidance of my staff. The C38 received my personal attention as the design progressed to completion. No prototype was used.

Displaced by the diesel-electric era, the C38 gradually descended to freight and less demanding passenger duties until December, 1970 when 3820 made the official last run of this gallant class. Fortunately, thanks to painstaking restoration and care carried out mainly by volunteers from the base at Eveleigh Workshops, 3801, operated by 3801 Limited and Powerhouse Museum's 3830 keep alive the spirit of one of Australia's greatest express steam locomotives.

To the north, steam in the 'fifties would enjoy its Indian summer on the narrow gauge Queensland Railways with the introduction of the BB18^1/$_4$ Australia's last Pacific class. First built in 1926 during Robert Chalmers period as CME, the original B18^1/$_4$ was regarded as one of the QR's two most successful designs, the C17 being the other. By 1947, the 'Betty's' as they were called (from their code 'bety' in telegraphic language) numbered a total of 83 hard-working locomotives.

With wartime trauma behind it, the QR's decision to equip with more main line passenger and general purpose motive power came down almost without argument on the side of Queensland's favourite engine. Except that the incumbent CME, Vincent Hall would grasp the opportunity to include the new technology development that had not been available to the first B18^1/$_4$ team. Roller bearings, longer travel valves, redesigned smokebox, cast wheel centres and larger tenders were among the features that distinguished the BB18^1/$_4$ the 170 psi boiler pressure went unchanged as did the 51-inch diameter driving wheels.[11] Though the BB was in many ways a new locomotive compared with its predecessor, the restricting factor of the QR's 12-ton axle load would still determine the advancement of a new design.

Authorisation was given in 1948 for 55 locomotives with construction divided between two hemispheres – 35 engines from Vulcan Foundry of Newton-le-Willows in England while Walkers Limited, of Maryborough held the residual contract. The English engines were unloaded on Brisbane wharves in 1951, but Walkers production, delayed until 1955, proved such an irritant that at one time it seemed the tide of railway business might turn against the State's traditional engine builder, but as history testifies the crisis was overcome.

Above and right: No. 1079 on the Sunshine Express 75th Anniversary train, from Cairns to Brisbane, 1999.

Inset: No 1079 builder's plate.

Dr Wilfred Brook

Resplendent in green boiler livery with deep red (carmine or vermillion) buffer beams and lining out, and chrome-plated steel boiler bands, the BB18^1/$_4$ carried the banner of steam's resurgence on the QR. With crisp exhaust, the new engines headed a 400-ton *Sunshine Express* and in favourable stretches their silver-tyred wheels could turn at 60 mph (96 kph). As track strengthening improved, on Central Queensland coal trains their loads reached 730 tons in the final days before 1970 when the QR went fully diesel. Walkers delivered no. 1089 from Maryborough workshops on 13 March, 1958. The waiting crowd cheered. It was not only the conclusion of the BB18^1/$_4$ order, but also the end of full size steam locomotive construction in Australia.

Note: No 1079 was not officially 'written off' at the coming dieselisation, being retained for special Heritage duty and, in that context, the BB18^1/$_4$ is the only Australian steam locomotive class not removed from the register. No 1079 continues to be maintained as part of the QR Heritage Collection; 1072 is operated by the Zig Zag Railway near Lithgow, New South Wales; 1089 is scheduled for restoration in QR workshops.

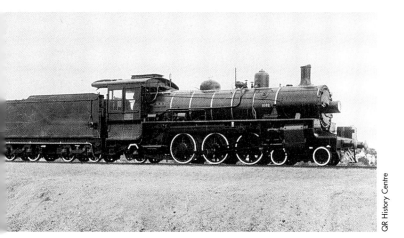

Loco

When I was a lad many years ago
How the smithy's furnace used to glow!
And the sweat on our foreheads used to gleam,
Back in the good old days of steam!
A man was a man, and knew his trade
And the destination of the parts he made.
We worked together as well-oiled team,
Back in the good old days of steam!

BB18¼ class no. 1089, last government steam loco built
in Australia, delivered by Walkers Ltd in March 1958.

George's Lament, from Sidetrack Theatre 1984

The 520 class looked like no other Australian locomotive when it was launched on the SAR's broad gauge metals in 1943. And apart from an arresting shark-like visage, the new 4-8-4 soon made its mark for speed, power and efficiency.

CHAPTER 10

LAST OF THE 16-WHEELERS
S.A.'s 520 CLASS

SAR/Author's collection

F rank Harrison was responsible for the design of only one steam locomotive during his relatively brief term as South Australia's CME, but it was a brilliantly successful design. The pity is that it came so late.

In fact, he may never have reached the top job except that State Premier, Tom Playford was moved to write to the Prime Minister, Ben Chifley asking for a clarification of the CME position.

At issue was Fred Shea's 'temporary' transfer from the SAR to a wartime post in the aircraft industry, and then another transfer to assist Harold Clapp with the national gauge standardization project. All this time Harrison had stood 'waiting in the wings'. As Playford said in his letter of 17 September, 1948 ...[1]

Referring to the appointment of Mr. Shea, at present on temporary duties with the Commonwealth, acting in an advisory capacity in connection with the uniform railway gauges, I would be very pleased if it would be possible for the Commonwealth to now give consideration to Mr. Shea's permanent appointment. This Officer was the Chief Mechanical Engineer at Islington at the outbreak of the War, and, at the request of the Commonwealth, he was made available to assist in the War effort in connection with aeroplane manufacture and repair. At the cessation of hostilities, he was transferred to unification of railway gauge work, and from time to time, has requested an extension of leave from our Department, with the purpose of ultimately taking up a permanent appointment with the Commonwealth. With the approval by the States of New South Wales, Victoria and South Australia to a unification agreement, there appears to be now no reason why this appointment should be further held in abeyance. Actually, I believe it has been approved for some two months, but not formally announced.

Frank Harrison, Chief Mechanical Engineer, South Australian Railways.

Our present Acting Chief Mechanical Engineer, Mr. F.H. Harrison, has received a most attractive offer from New South Wales, and he naturally is anxious to know what his ultimate position would be, as he does not wish to revert to the position of Workshop Manager. He has a week in which to make a decision as to whether he would accept the New South Wales proposal, and, as you can easily see, if he does accept this proposal, it would mean that South Australia would probably ultimately lose the services of both her Officers – one to private industry, and the other to the Commonwealth Service.

I realize that you are extremely busy at this time, but would be very

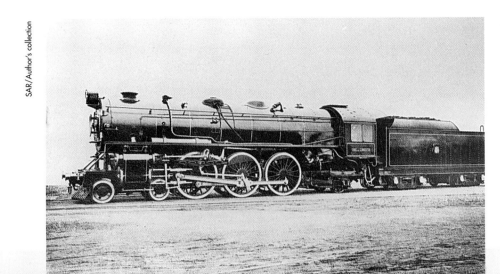

SAR/Author's collection

Left: The handsome 600 class of the Webb era.

Below: Islington Workshops, rebuilt during the Webb-Shea years into a modern manufacturing facility which produced 710, 720 and 520 classes.

SAR/Author's collection

Three ages of broad gauge steam on the SAR - from left, the veteran Rx class 4-6-0, centre – the 1943-era 520 class 4-8-4 and right

e 620 class light Pacific, a Fred Shea engine of 1936.

P.A. Butler/Author's collection

grateful if you could confer with the Minister for Transport to have Mr. Shea's appointment ratified.

Nine days later, Prime Minister Chifley gave Playford his answer, [2] referring to 'our talk in Adelaide, and your letter of the 17th Sept., I discussed with Mr. Ward (Federal Transport Minister) the question of Mr. Shea's appointment'...

As I indicated to you, I had already approved of Mr. Shea's appointment to the Commonwealth, but on discussing the position with Mr. Ward, I find that the Regulations covering the Agreement, which would also embody the appointment, has been held up due to the Agreement not being signed by New South Wales.

I am taking the opportunity to-day of seeing Mr. McKell (NSW Premier) regarding the matter, but you can take it as definite that subject to the electors decision on Saturday we propose to appoint Mr. Shea to the Commonwealth Service.

The title of 'acting' was smartly removed. One might comment that not too many railwaymen have their promotion confirmed by the joint action of a Prime Minister and State Premier.

Though, obviously, they were many miles apart and of different gauges, broad and standard, yet significantly close in certain important specifications, some observers have been bold enough to compare the virtues of a 520 with a C38; a warning, the following remarks may possibly offend. [3]

'The 520 is the sort of locomotive New South Wales could or should have attempted,' said the late John Buckland, one of the most respected railway historians.

'The SAR 520 class ... an engine that in view of some of us connoisseurs ought to have more praise lavished on it than the C38,' wrote loco buff Clive Huggan who grew up amid South Australia's big power years.

And to quote Harry Haynes, a retired senior driver who spent 30 years on the footplate in South Australia: 'The 520, which puts out 2300 horsepower, is a unique locomotive in that it is both coal and oil fired – there's not many of them left in the world. I'd have to say that the later models of the 520 are a better locomotive than the New South Wales C38 which is viewed by many as the best steam loco in Australia'. Harry ended the interview with a grin, saying 'There ya go, that'll get up the nose of some

PDSRM

Assembly of 520 brings boiler and wheels together at Islington Workshops in 1943 and reveals the shape of the U.S.-inspired 'shark' or 'chisel' nose as the feature came to be known.

New South drivers'. [4]

Yet, on home ground, one has to note that the ARHS *Bulletin* of March 1943 advised members to exercise caution in accepting extravagant press claims for the power, size and speed of the C38. The *Bulletin* continued: 'It must be pointed out that this class of locomotive is not especially outstanding in comparison with some of the new productions of other States'.

The point is that both the C38, a 4-6-2 and the 520, a 4-8-4 excelled at the tasks they were built to perform. Injecting more power and speed into running the increasingly heavy Limiteds, Expresses and Daylights was Harold Young's objective, and the no-nonsense Scot CME achieved his purpose. Introducing a locomotive with power and speed to operate equally well with passenger or freight trains over medium weight track was the other man's objective, and the young engineer who could not yet call himself 'CME' equally achieved his purpose.

Harrison began the 520 drawings in 1940 while still wearing his 'acting' sash. He was an individualist, for he chose the American (sometimes 'Northern') 4-8-4 wheel arrangement which, except for Victoria's lone H220 and the SAR's 500B had not been selected (and would not be) by any other Australian railway. But on its 16 wheels the 520 proved fleet of foot, with its well balanced 5ft 6in driving wheels effortlessly reeling off 70 mph (112 kph), while a 15-ton axle load carried it without restriction across the 60 lb plant of the SAR's lighter Murray Lands branches. A boiler pressure of 215 lbs and a 31,600 lb tractive effort gave it ample power to handle express passenger and fast freight regardless.[5] Bradford Kendall's foundry in Sydney was responsible for the cast steel bar frames. The 12-wheel variable capacity tender contained sufficient fuel space (9^1/$_2$ tons of coal and 9100 gallons of water maximum) to cover the 134 miles (216 km) between Adelaide and Port Pirie non-stop; on light lines the fuel load could be reduced to a fixed level.

Commissioner Anderson authorised the building of number 520 in December 1941.[6] It was the month of Japan's southward march and in the critical years of the Pacific War that followed, every available SAR loco would be called out to handle the wartime traffic. Islington Workshops delivered 520 for a media inspection at Adelaide Station on 26 October, 1943 and a month later it was in service. Second engine 521 appeared in the following February; during tests with a 510 ton load, it developed 2600 IHP and clocked 78 mph (124 kph) while enginemen yarned that the speed could have gone higher.

Reporting the media inspection at Adelaide Station, the *Advertiser* commented that 'the most modern feature of the new locomotive is that little, if any, smoke will be seen, and there will be a complete absence of sparks'. The 520, named *Thomas Playford*, was capable of running between Adelaide and Port Pirie or Terowie without stopping to refuel. The Premier (Mr. Playford) drove the engine along the Islington Workshops siding and enjoyed 'a personal experience of an innovation in cabin accommodation. The driver and fireman have upholstered seats in a cabin about four times

Late Lionel Bates/Lloyd Holmes collection

No. 525, Sir
Willoughby Norrie
*drifts through the hills
at Upper Sturt with an
Adelaide-bound local
train from Bridgewater.*

the size of the usual engine cabin. Doors and windows are fitted as in the best luxury carriages.' [7]

The 520 was not only an impressive performer, it also looked impressive. When he decided on streamlining, Harrison at first had in mind the bulbous nose of a Norfolk and Western Railroad J class, until he picked up a copy of *Railway Age* and saw a picture of the Pennsylvania Railroad's new T1 Duplex with sleek lines and chisel front, the work of leading American stylist Raymond Loewy. 'Copy this' (or words to that effect) he memoed to his Design Office.

Retired railway engineer, Bill Holmesby (who spent 44 years with the South Australian and Commonwealth railways) and knew the CME's family, recalled…

Frank was able to stamp his authority on the 520, insisting on a clean, streamlined appearance. I know he spent hours with the design staff on these features – and he wanted the inclusion of the latest accessories. With his redesign of the 520's front end shape, it has been rightly said that Frank produced the most impressive of all Australian steam locomotives. [8]

Finished in a livery of Hawthorn green and lined-out in cream, the handsome 520 seemed to signify that steam power could be as modern as they came and never likely to be shaken from its throne. Seven of the 200-ton locomotives were in Islington's first order, until 526 was completed in June, 1945. Most of them were named after prominent men of their time. Number 520 was *Sir Malcolm Barclay-Harvey*, the State Governor and something of a railway buff himself. [9]

On day Harrison called in his clerk and said 'Find out for me where Barclay-Harvey is'. The clerk disappeared and an hour later appeared with a worried look. 'I rang Government House, sir', he said, 'and Parliament House, but no one seems to know where the Governor is'. The CME winced. 'Stone the crows, Jack', he replied. 'I didn't mean the Governor, I meant the bloody engine!'

Born in Port Augusta in 1899, seventh son of a railway family – his father was an express train guard – Frank Hugh Harrison entered the railways as an apprentice fitter and turner and after a spectacular scholarship-winning academic career, in 1926 was appointed the young Works Manager at Islington where under the Webb-Shea regime he would be responsible for the 'hands on' task of lifting the near moribund plant into the 20th century. He was in charge of Islington's aircraft production during the war and also South Australia's part in the ASG program. Technical Assistant to the Commonwealth Railways was another role he filled. He made two overseas tours, in 1926-28 and again in 1944-45, studying latest developments in workshops and locomotive operation. [10]

The 520 – converted to standard gauge it might have run the Trans-Australian Express – but dieselisation intervened.

Rail-lore has it that the boy from Islington was determined, once given the CME authority, to deliver a locomotive as good as – if not better – than anything Fred Shea had fathered. He didn't disappoint.

Shea's last design, the 620 light Pacific, smaller than the 520, was an able performer yet in tests along the South line with equivalent trains, the

520's coal consumption (very important for the coal-importing SAR) substantially undercut the 620 to the extent of 20-30%. The Webb-Shea big 600 Pacific was operationally limited by a 23-ton axle load; the 520 at almost eight tons less could haul loads close to the 600's rating without much route restriction.

North of Redhill, the 520 was permitted 70 mph (112 kph) on passenger trains. On one memorable occasion, a delayed Trans-Australian Express meant a tight, if not impossible connection with the Melbourne-bound *Overland* for the SAR train standing at Port Pirie Station. Behind 523 (*Essington Lewis*) the East-West Express whistled out and the next 134 miles it covered in just 149 minutes. With a vital half hour saved, 523 pulled into Adelaide Station to send its grateful passengers across to the waiting *Overland*.

As a relatively young and highly qualified engineer, Harrison was perceived to be impatient with

Belair is a stopping place of class-leader 520 on a misty morning in the Adelaide Hills

W.M. Bailey/National Library

PDSRM

The enclosed cab of a 520 class which brought a new degree of comfort to the footplate crew.

the attitudes (or imagined attitudes) of a senior 'old guard'. His style of management came to be regarded as autocratic and unpopular with numerous staff; it was a brave (or foolish) man who would contest a CME decision.[11]   In the King's Birthday Honours of June, 1944, he received the OBE. The press noted that Mr Harrison was responsible for the mechanical well-being of a Railway Department which represented a £31 million capital investment

SAR/Author's collection

and employed a staff of close on 10,000 people.

No. 525, Sir Mellis Napier

Clearly he was not afraid of innovation. His was *belongs to the batch of the* the first Australian locomotive to have roller bearings on *520 class distinguished from* all wheels, to have an all-welded steel firebox. Weight- *nos. 520-522 by an improved* saving welding was employed extensively in putting *nose design intended to lift* together the frames, cast steel cylinder assemblies, cabs, *the smoke exhaust.* trailing trucks and tender. Lateral motion devices were fitted to the leading driving and trailing truck axles. A steam jet located within the firebox was designed to heighten combustion and reduce the density of smoke emission. Drivers enjoyed the roomy and totally enclosed cab, but not so the sweating firemen until the mining shut-downs of the late 1940s introduced the SAR's particular system of oil and oil-coal firing.

Five more locomotives were completed in 1947 and except for the original first three, all 520s appeared in a livery of solid black with silver lining-out. Important modifications were made to the front streamlining after No. 522 to improve the smoke-lifting performance, and giving the following engines a rather 'sharper' appearance. Plans to build a further eight locomotives did not proceed and by 1971 all 12 were out of service. Nor did the Commonwealth Railways persist in adapting the 520 to standard gauge on six ft driving wheels (and a 16-wheel tender holding 17

Author's photograph

Ode to a Diesel

On the road to Santa Fe
Where the flying diesels play.
Rootin', tootin' on their whistles
as they claim the right of way.
Hear them screaming for the crossing
Dashing past the old steam pots
Stand aside, you puffing billies
We can't wait while you get hot.

Fred Shea, in USA, 1951

Author's photograph

tons of coal and 18,000 gallons of water) as replacement power for the Trans-Australian Express.

What a pity the 520 came so late.

Harrison introduced the first of the English Electric diesels (named *Lady Norrie*) in September 1951 and accepted that Islington would build no more steam. With that decision went his plan for the heavy 800 class which would have been a replacement for the ageing 500B.

Dissatisfied with the line of promotion to Commissionership – the chair traditionally went to the Chief Civil Engineer – he resigned in August, 1952 to join a firm of combustion engineers, Pascoe & Co, of Woodville, as general manager. The Commissioner regretted the departure of a fine engineer who had given 13 years' service as CME. At the age of 58, sudden death on 7 November, 1957 ended the life of the man who had ushered in one of Australia's most striking and successful steam locomotives.[12]

The eight named locomotives were 520 *Sir Malcolm Barclay-Harvey*, 521 *Thomas Playford*, 522 *Malcolm McIntosh*, 523 *Essington Lewis*, 524 *Sir Mellis Napier*, 525 *Sir Willoughby Norrie*, 526 *Duchess of Gloucester*, 527 *C.B. Anderson*.

520, currently awaiting repair has been operated by Steam Ranger between Mt. Barker and Victor Harbour. 523 is a static exhibit at the Port Dock Station Railway Museum, Port Adelaide.

Above: The driver's corner of 523's cab at Port Dock Station Railway Museum

Below: No. 526, Duchess of Gloucester *preparing for duty with the Mile End coaling tower looming behind it. Coal was an inseparable commodity at every Australian loco depot.*

Douglas Colquhoun/Lloyd Holmes collection

Port Pirie on 6 September 1970 was the scene of a rare meeting between two locomotives that embodied the finest and final development of Australian-made express steam power. South Australian 526, Duchess of Gloucester *stands to the left on broad gauge tracks while 3813 waits alongside on the standard gauge rails that have brought it from New South Wales.*

Late R.B. McMillan collection/ARHS Resource Centre

What a sight it was!

The 38 class Pacific engine ranged alongside 520 class engine, both engines being the pride of the N. S. W. G. R. and S. A. R. respectively. It was a sight I'll never forget as long as I live. It was a sight that would gladden the heart of any true Railwayman. The 38 class bedecked in her green paint and yellow stripes with the N. S. W. coat of arms on the tender, the 520 with her streamlined nose, shiny black paint and silver stripes, both lined up as though they were to have a race, and what a race it would have been, if it had at all been possible![13]

From Driver Jack McKay recalling the day he drove the N.S.W. visitor, 3813 between Port Pirie and Peterborough in September 1970.

PRINCIPAL LOCOMOTIVE DIMENSIONS

Conversion formulae

1 in = 25.4 mm	1 kg = 2.2 lbs
1 ft = 304.8 mm	1 ton = 2240 lbs = 1.016 tonnes
1 m = 3.28 ft	1 tonne = 2205 lbs
1 sq ft = .093 sq m	1 kilonewton = 225 lbs
1 sq m = 10.76 sq ft	1 lb/sq in (psi) = 6.90 kilopascals
1 mile = 1.61 km	1 kg/sq cm = 14.2 psi
1 km = .62 mile	1 hp = .746 kilowatts (kw)
1 lb = .45 kg	1 kw = 1.34 hp

Grades

1-in-100 is 1 ft rise in 100 ft horizontally;

1-in-50 is 1 ft rise in 50 ft horizontally, etc.

Percentage grades are the rise in 100 ft.

Tractive Effort

The normal figure quoted for steam locos is the 'starting' or 'rated' tractive effort; calculated by the formula – for 2-cylinder engines:

$$\text{T.E. (lbs)} = \frac{\text{Cylinder diameter (in)}^2 \times \text{Stroke (in)} \times 85\% \text{ Boiler pressure (psi)}}{\text{Driving wheel diameter (in)}}$$

The % boiler pressure is usually taken as 80% for saturated steam engines and 85% for superheated.

For 3-cylinder engines multiply by 1.5 and for 4-cylinder by 2. Maximum starting tractive effort is limited by wheel adhesion to about 25% of the total axle load of the drivers. This in turn is limited by rail weight, track and bridge strength.

Chapter 1

Class H (No.220) 4-8-4
Victorian Railways

Principal dimensions

	Imperial	Metric
Cylinders (3)	$21^1/_2$ x 28 in	551 x 711 mm
Coupled wheels	5 ft 7 in	1702 mm
Boiler pressure	220 lb	1517 kPa
Grate area	68 sq ft	6.3 m²
Heating surface (total)		
	4760 sq ft	442.2 m²
Tractive effort	55,008 lb	244.8 kN
Axle load	23.5 tons	23.8 tonnes
Weight (total)	260 tons	265.1 tonnes
Gauge	5 ft 3 in	1600 mm
Tender		
Coal	9 tons	9 tonnes
Water	14,000 gals	63,644 litres
Built:	1941 Newport 1	
Preserved:	H220 Railway Museum, North Williamstown	

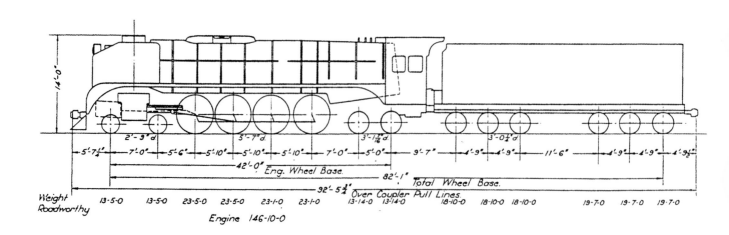

Chapter 2

Class 720, 2-8-4
South Australian Railways

Principal dimensions

	Imperial	Metric
Cylinders (2)	22 x 28 in	559 x 711 mm
Coupled wheels	4 ft 9 in	1448 mm
Boiler pressure	215 lb	1481 kPa
Grate area	46.8 sq ft	4.384 m²
Heating surface (total)		
	2975 sq ft	276.37 m²
Tractive effort *	43,450 lb	193.4 kN
Axle load	19.2 tons	19.8 tonnes
Weight (total	227.4 tons	232 tonnes
Gauge	5 ft 3 in	1600 mm
Tender		
Coal	17 tons	17.4 tonnes
Water	9400 gal	43,000 litres
Built:	1930-43 Islington 17	
Preserved:	Nil	

* Booster added 8600 lbs tractive effort

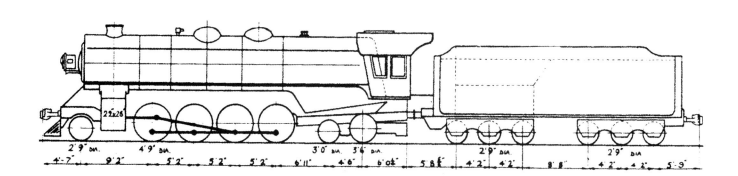

Chapter 3

Class C, 4-6-0
Commonwealth Railways

Principal dimensions

	Imperial	Metric
Cylinders (2)	23 x 26 in	584 x 660 mm
Coupled wheels	5 ft 9 in	17.53 mm
Boiler pressure	180 lb	1241 kPa
Grate area	30.5 sq ft	2.833 m²
Heating surface (total)		
	2640 sq ft	245.26 m²
Tractive effort	30,500 lb	135.7 kN
Axle load	20.3 tons	20.48 tonnes
Weight (total)	207 tons	211.1 tonnes
Gauge	4 ft 8¹/₂ in	1435 mm
Tender		
Coal	17 tons	17.5 tonnes
Water	12,180 gals	56,360 litres
Built:	1938 Walkers 8	
Preserved:	Nil	

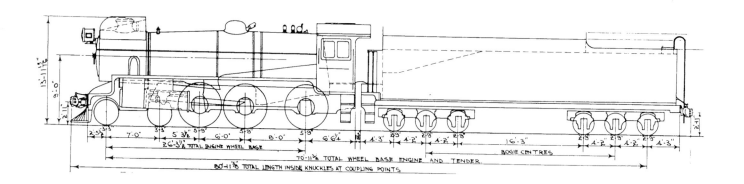

Chapter 4

Class AD60, 4-8-4 + 4-8-4
New South Wales Government Railways

Principal dimensions

	Imperial	Metric
Cylinders (4)	$19^1/_4$ x 26 in	489 x 660 mm
Coupled wheels	4 ft 7 in	1397 mm
Boiler pressure	200 lb	1379 kPa
Grate area	63.5 sq ft	5.899 m²
Heating surface (total)		
	3780 sq ft	351.17 m²
Tractive effort*	59,559 lb	265 kN
Axle load	16.5 tons	16.76 tonnes
Weight (total)	263.5 tons	269 tonnes
Gauge	4 ft 8$^1/_2$ in	1435 mm
Bunker/Tanks		
Coal	14 tons	14.2 tonnes
Water	9350 gals	42,500 litres
Built:	1952-57 Beyer Peacock (Manchester) 42	
Preserved:	6029 ARHS Museum, Canberra (for future operation);	
	also 6039, Dorrigo Rail Museum;	
	6040, Rail Transport Museum, Thirlmere;	
	6042, Forbes Vintage Village.	

* On 30 modified Garratts with $19^7/_8$in. cylinders, increased to 63,016 lb (280.4 kN); coal capacity increased to 18 tons; axle load to 18 tons. Total weight to 264 tons/268 tonnes.

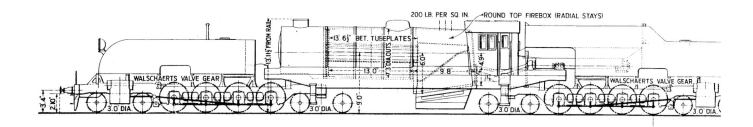

Chapter 6

Class C19, 4-8-0
Queensland Railways

Principal dimensions

	Imperial	Metric
Cylinders (2)	19 x 23 in	403 x 584 mm
Coupled wheels	4 ft 0 in	1219 mm
Boiler pressure	160 lb	1103 kPa
Grate area	21.4 sq ft	1.985 m²
Heating surface (total)		
	1206 sq ft	112.03m²
Tractive effort	23,525 lb	104.7kN
Axle load	10 tons	10 tonnes
Weight (total	97 tons	98.6 tonnes
Gauge	3 ft 6 in	1067 mm
Tender		
Coal	11 tons	11.2 tonnes
Water	3500 gal	15,910 litres
Built	1922-35 Ipswich 20, Walkers 6, plus 3 CC19 converted from C18 (Ipswich).	
Preserved:	700 QR Heritage Collection	

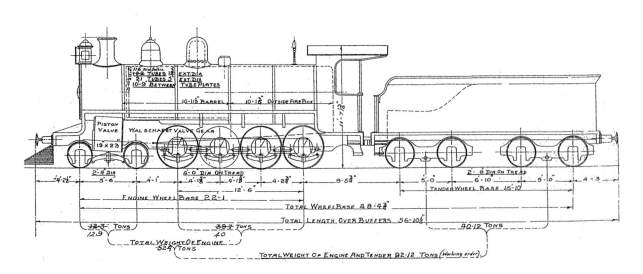

Chapter 7

Class S, 4-8-2
Western Australian Government Railways

Principal dimensions

	Imperial	Metric
Cylinders (2)	19 x 24 in	483 x 610 mm
Coupled wheels	4 ft 0 in	1219 mm
Boiler pressure	200 lb	1379 kPa
Grate area	40 sq ft	3.716 m^2
Heating surface (total)		
	2121 sq ft	197.04 m^2
Tractive effort	30,685 lb	136.6 kN
Axle load	13 tons	13.2 tonnes
Weight (total)	119 tons	121.4 tonnes
Gauge	3 ft 6 in	1067 mm
Tender*		
Coal	9 tons	9 tonnes
Water	3500 gals	15,910 litres

Built: 1943-47 Midland 10

Preserved: 542, ARHS Operational, 547 Bellarine Peninsula
                  Railway (Vic), 549 East Perth Station.

*Later changed on five locos to 7 tons and 5000 gals.

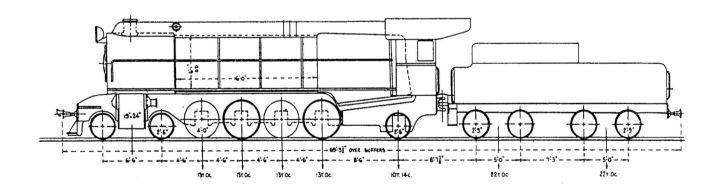

Chapter 8

Class Q, 4-8-2
Tasmanian Government Railways

Principal dimensions

	Imperial	Metric
Cylinders (2)	20 x 24 in	508 x 610 mm
Coupled wheel	4 ft 0 in	1219 mm
Boiler pressure	160 lb	1103 kPa
Grate area	32.5 sq ft	3.019 m²
Heating surface	1592 sq ft	147.89 m²
Tractive effort	27,200 lb	121 kN
Axle load	12.5 tons	12.8 tonnes
Weight (total)	104 tons	105.6 tonnes
Gauge	3 ft 6 in	1067 mm
Tender		
Coal	6 tons	6 tonnes
Water	3500 gal	15,910 litres
Built:	1922-45 Perry 6, Walkers 3, Clyde 10	
Preserved:	Q5 Tasmanian Transport Museum, Glenorchy	

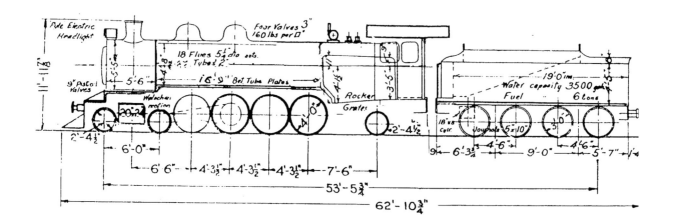

Chapter 9

Class C38, 4-6-2
New South Wales Government Railways
Principal Dimensions

	Imperial	Metric
Driving wheels	5 ft 9 in	1753mm
Cylinders	21^1/$_2$ x 26 in	546 x 660mm
Pressure	245 lb	1689 kPa
Grate area	47 sq ft	4.366 m^2
Heating Surface	3367 sq ft	312.88 m^2
Axle load	22t 12cwt	23 tonnes
Weight	195 tons	198.1 tonnes
Streamlined	201 tons	204.2 tonnes
Tractive effort	36,200 lb	161.4 kN
Gauge	4 ft 8^1/$_2$ in	1435 mm
Tender		
Coal	14 tons	14.2 tonnes
Water	8100 gal	36, 823 litres

Built 1943-9   Clyde 5, Eveleigh 13, Cardiff 12

3801, leased by the 3801 organisation and 3830, owned by the Powerhouse
Museum are both in operation.

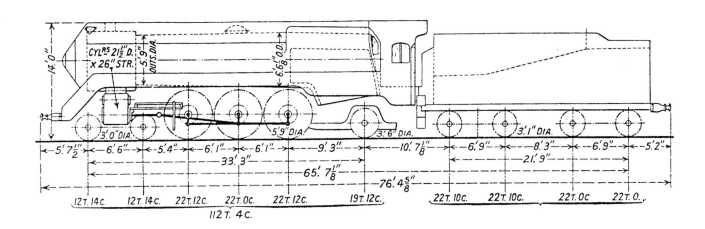

Chapter 9 continued

Class BB18$^1/_4$, 4-6-2
Queensland Railways
Principal Dimensions

	Imperial	Metric
Driving Wheels	4 ft 3 in	1295 mm
Cylinders	18$^1/_4$ x 24 in	464 x 610 mm
Pressure	170 lb	1172 kPa
Grate	25 sq ft	2.323 m^2
Axle load	12 tons	12.05 tonnes
Weight	101 tons	102.6 tonnes
Tractive effort	22,650 lb	100.8 kN
Gauge	3 ft 6 in	1067mm

Built 1951-58 Vulcan 35, Walkers 20

BB18$^1/_4$ 1079 is maintained as part of the QR Heritage Collection; 1072 is operated by the Zig Zag Railway near Lithgow, New South Wales; 1089 is scheduled for restoration in QR workshops.

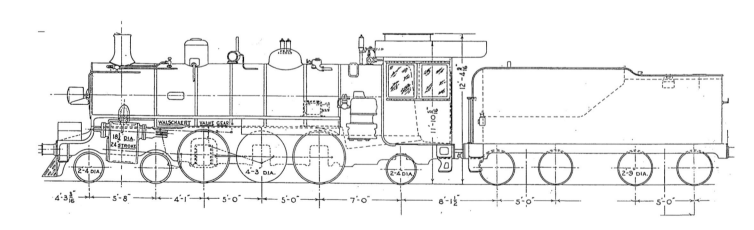

Chapter 10

Class 520, 4-8-4
South Australian Railways
Principal Dimensions

	Imperial	Metric
Driving wheels	5 ft 6 in	1676 mm
Cylinders	20 x 28 in	521 x 711 mm
Pressure	215 lb	1482 kPa
Grate area	46 sq ft	4.181 m²
Axle load	15t 12c	16.05 tonnes
Weight	200 tons	203.9 tonnes
Tractive effort	32,600 lb	145 kN
Gauge	5 ft 3 in	1600mm

Built 1943-7   Islington 12

The eight named locomotives were 520 Sir Malcolm Barclay-Harvey,
521 Thomas Playford, 522 Malcolm McIntosh, 523 Essington Lewis,
524 Sir Mellis Napier, 525 Sir Willoughby Norrie, 526 Duchess of Gloucester,
527 C.B. Anderson.

520, currently under repair has been operated by Steam Ranger between
Mount Barker and Victor Harbour. 523 is a static exhibit at the Port Dock
Station Museum, Port Adelaide.

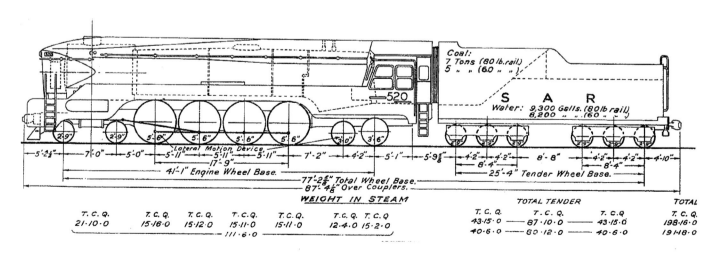

Principal locomotive dimensions

STEAMING FROM AFAR

In concluding a survey of the survivors in steam, it would be crass indeed to ignore the fine and 'big' locomotives brought from overseas that have also escaped the oxy-torch. In the decade following the end of World War II, government railways and private industry were congested with overdue maintenance, repairs and in some instances, engaged in a building program. The workshops problem, together with a considerable skilled labour shortage meant that the urgent need for new locomotives could not be locally met. In the main, the traditional British firms stood to reap the reward of a harvest that numbered in excess of 380 locomotives.

Beyer, Peacock, a builder which since last century had exported hundreds of engines to Australia makes a good case study. In 1946 the Victorian Railways approached Beyer, Peacock to design an express Garratt locomotive with a 19-ton axle load for the Western line (replacing the role intended for H220). Mr Cyril Williams, Sales Director of the Manchester company politely replied that Beyer, Peacock would answer the VR's inquiry – though with undisguised scepticism and reluctance. Williams was someone who well understood the railway market for in the past he had been the Australian representative of British locomotive manufacturers. Over some 20 years, he hastened to point out, his company had spent a small fortune in time, money and manpower supplying drawings and quotes for Australian engines which never left the drawing board.

One can understand Williams' lack of enthusiasm. The VR had entertained ideas of acquiring a broad gauge Garratt in the early 1920s, but Beyer, Peacock's booby prize was the two narrow gauge G class of 1926. Tasmania, where the whole Garratt saga had begun, placed its last government order in 1912. And so it went on – three for the Emu Bay, two for the Fyansford cement private line, an M and Ms trickle in Western Australia. Nibbles from Queensland stretched over 30 years (1911, 1921, 1925, 1937 by way of example) for the Main Range climb. And most of all, the frustrating prize target of New South Wales; four different stillborn prospects since 1920, culminating in 1948 when Harold Young had come close to winning the large 'Algerian' Garratt for Southern line expresses.

So, with the advent of the 1950s Beyer, Peacock must have thought that – suddenly, after these untold lean years – all its Christmases had come at once. In the hurry to engine-up, three major orders arrived from Australia between 1949 and 1952. For Queensland, blessedly not deterred by the ASG imbroglio, 30 Beyer-Garratts. For South Australia, 10 – a contract that had to be switched to the Societe Franco-Belge because of Manchester's glut of work. And for New South Wales, 25 – these to be among the largest and most advanced articulateds that the Company would ever build; an order soon to be doubled! Only in Western Australia did Beyer, Peacock fail in its bid to sell a Garratt, the proposed VG (heavy) and WG (light) classes, possibly up to 50 locomotives, though it picked up a consolation prize in building 60 of the fine 4-8-2 W class.

Other manufacturers could report the same spurt in business. North British held contracts to supply 35 of the Pm/Pmr Pacifics to Western Australia and 70 R class Hudsons to Victoria. Vulcan Foundry was engaged in making eight H class Mountain type for Tasmania, 60 of the 2-8-0 high-boilered J class for Victoria and 35 BB18^1/$_4$ for Queensland, Robert Stephenson and Hawthorns had in progress the 10 Tasmanian M class Pacifics to be followed by 24 of the large V class 2-8-2s for Western Australia. Some of these locomotives were of a typical 'international' design – an earlier cousin of the H class could be found on the railways of Ghana in North Africa, duplicates of the M class worked on the Indian metre gauge, and by and large the Garratts belonged to the world. In contrast, the VR set the specifications of its express 4-6-4 and the light line J, the latter 2-8-0 being Victoria's final steam power.

All of these classes have a locomotive (or locomotives) back in steam, or in progress of restoration. Brief descriptions of their size and power are given on the following pages. (Worth noting is that America's only contribution to the post-war steam bonanza was the 20 light Mikado D59 class for New South Wales. But it represented a picture that would reverse itself dramatically in the next couple of decades when the diesel-electric invasion began).

At its peak after World War 2, Australian steam numbered around 3500 locomotives. Today some 50 remain in service and for that small mercy, all who cherish the memory of the iron horse should be grateful.

1950 Beyer Garratt 4-8-2 + 2-8-4 Queensland

Despite resistance to operating the Australian Standard Garratt (ASG) during World War 2, the Queensland Railways went ahead post-war with an order for 30 of the articulated types – 10 from Beyer, Peacock, and 20 by an associated builder, Franco-Belge of France. These fine maroon-liveried locos arrived in 1950 and were used initially on passenger and freight trains based at Rockhampton, but soon appeared more widely throughout the system. Problems were experienced with excessive heat conditions for enginemen in tunnels, and to some extent operations were restricted. The advent of diesel power meant concentration on heavy export coal traffic in the Dawson Valley, which was to be the last major task for the Beyer- Garratts – in all a short working life. They were removed from the register between 1964 and 1970.

Principal dimensions

Driving wheels	4 ft 3 in	1295 mm
Cylinders (4)	$13^3/4$ x 26 in	337 x 660 mm
Pressure	200 lb	1379 kPa
Weight	137 tons	139.2 tonnes
Tractive effort	32,770 lb	145.8 kN
Gauge	3 ft 6 in	1067 mm

Built: 1950 30 locomotives

Preserved: Beyer-Garratt 1009 is maintained operable as part of the QR Heritage Collection.

Author's photograph

1951 R Class 4-6-4 Victoria

Late J.L. Buckland/Author's collection

Intended to replace the ageing A2 class on fast passenger services, the 70 Hudson type R class were built by the North British Locomotive Co. of Scotland from 1951–54. First considered as a Pacific (4-6-2) they appeared as a 4-6-4 – the only class of tender locomotive in Australia with the Hudson wheel arrangement.

The design included a mechanical stoker and roller-bearing axle boxes on both locomotive and tender, as well as SCOA-P type driving wheels to facilitate the possibility of conversion to standard gauge. After minor problems, the R class settled in as an efficient, fast-moving machine. Introduction of diesel power displaced them from the main passenger services such as the *Overland*, yet they performed effectively on freight trains.

Two were fitted for oil firing in 1955-7 and one equipped with Stug brown-coal-burning apparatus in 1956, but converted back to conventional fuel three years later. The R began to be withdrawn in the early 1960s after a comparatively short life.

Principal dimensions

Driving wheels	6 ft 1 in	1853 mm
Cylinders	21¹/₂ x 28 in	546 x 711 mm
Pressure	210lb	1448 kPa
Weight	187 tons	190 tonnes
Tractive effort	31,648 lb	140.8 kN
Gauge	5 ft 3 in	1600 mm

Built: 1951-2 70 locomotives

Preserved: Nos 700 (awaiting repair), 707, 711, 761 and 766 are operated by a variety of rail and enthusiast organisations.

1951 M class 4-6-2 Tasmania

Among the latter day importations of steam power, the M class stands out as quite a strong survivor. Intended for Tasmania's main line passenger traffic, 10 M class Pacifics were ordered from the U.K. builder, Robert Stephenson and Hawthorns in 1951. Together with the larger H class Mountain type assigned to freight duty, all were in service by 1952 though oncoming dieselisation would mean a relatively short working life.

Weighing 97 tons and with a 180 lb pressure boiler, the M closely resembled the metric gauge XB Pacific of the Indian Railways, just as the H was a repeat of pre-war Vulcan Foundry machines supplied to the railways of Ghana. Fitting of the 4 ft driving wheels taken from redundant Australian Standard Garratts increased the haulage power of the Pacifics and transformed the four converted locomotives to MA classification. Several of these trim passenger engines are to be found in Tasmania (as are survivors of the H class), some in steam-worthy condition. M6 has the distinction of being shipped to the mainland for operation on the Bellarine Peninsula Railway out of Queenscliff, Victoria.

Principal dimensions

Driving wheels	4 ft 7 in	1397mm
Cylinders	16 x 24 in	406 x 610mm
Pressure	180lb	1241kPa
Weight	96^1/$_2$ tons	98 tonnes
Tractive effort	17090 lbs	76 kN
Gauge	3 ft 6 in	1067mm

Built: 1952 10 locomotives

D.H. Jones photograph

1951 H class 4-8-2 Tasmania

When time could not be spared to evolve a new design, the TGR agreed to buy a locomotive type which had been supplied earlier to the African Gold Coast. Vulcan Foundry delivered the eight H class in 1951. Once again it was an instance of a capable steam locomotives arriving at about the same time as rival diesel power. However the H was used to advantage on the Main, Fingal and Western lines and later in the north-west.

D.H. Jones photograph

Two were out of service by 1962 and the rest joined them prematurely on the scrap track. Two were refurbished for the TGR's centenary celebrations in 1971 and one retained for enthusiast excursions.

Principal dimensions

Driving wheels	4 ft 0 in	1219 mm
Cylinders	18 x 24 in	457 x 610 mm
Pressure	200 lb	1379 kPa
Weight	111 tons	112.8 tonnes
Tractive effort	27,540 lb	122.6 kN
Gauge	3 ft 6 in	1067 mm
Built:	1951 8 locomotives	

Preserved: H2 operated by the Derwent Valley Railway
Preservation group is under refurbishment and expected to resume service.

1951 W class 4-8-2 Western Australia

Part of Western Australia's final steam modernization program, the 60 W class proved very effective locomotives on freight and passenger duties. Designed and built by Beyer, Peacock in 1951-2, they were able to handle heavy loads at a good average speed and were popular with crews for riding characteristics, power reverse and roller-bearing axleboxes. The same design was adopted by the Silverton Tramway Co. for their four semi-streamlined locomotives, also known as W class.

These Beyer, Peacock machines were not quickly supplanted by the diesels and first withdrawals waited until 1970. Within several years, however, virtually all the class had been scrapped except that several were retained for display and operation.

Principal dimensions

Driving wheels	4 ft 0 in	1219 mm
Cylinders	16 x 24 in	406 x 610 mm
Pressure	200 lb	1379 kPa
Weight	101 tons	102.6 tonnes
Tractive effort	21,760 lb	96.8 kN
Gauge	3 ft 6 in	1067 mm

Built: 1951-2 60 locomotives

Preserved: 903, 908, 920 and 945 are operated by the Hotham Valley Railway from Pinjarra; 931, 933 and 934 by the Pichi Richi Railway at Quorn; 901 and 907 by Steamtown at Peterborough; South Australia. 924 works on the MacDonnell Siding line of the Ghan Preservation Society near Alice Springs, Northern Territory.

Author's collection

1955 V class 2-8-2 Western Australia

In the very swansong of steam, the massive V-class locomotives were unloaded at Fremantle docks in 1955-6. C.W.Clarke, Assistant Commissioner (Engineering) of the Western Australian Government Railways set the specifications for the 24 engines.

Built to a Beyer, Peacock design by Robert Stephenson and Hawthorns Limited for heavy coal haulage, they were equipped with roller bearings, thermic syphons and power reverse. Grate area measures 40 sq ft (3.72 m²). These impressive locos gave excellent service, at first on coal trains and later on heavy freights along the Great Southern and South-West routes. The last V was officially retired on Christmas Eve 1971.

Principal dimensions

Driving wheels	4 ft 3 in	1295 mm
Cylinders	19 x 26 in	483 x 660 mm
Pressure	215 lb	1482 kPa
Weight	134 tons	136.7 tonnes
Tractive effort	33,633 lb	149.6 kN
Gauge	3 ft 6 in	1067 mm
Built:	1955-6 24 locomotives	

Preserved: V class 1213, owned privately by Ian Willis, operates from Pemberton and is at times engaged in revenue-earning log haulage on the line to Lyall Siding. V1220 is at the ARHS Bassendean Museum; V1209 is stored at the Bellarine Peninsula Railway, Victoria.

REFERENCES

CHAPTER ONE

1. For VR locomotive developments leading up to the S class, readers may refer to the career of A.E. Smith, CME, in the author's *Kings of the Iron Horse* (see bibliography).

2 The *VR Magazine* in March 1929 noted the completion at Newport Workshops of the third S class, the first heavy X class Mikado (10 more to be completed during the year) and that construction had begun on the first of six petrol-electric railmotors and trailers. 'By June or thereabouts nine more electric goods locomotives should be completed and in October the creation of 10 new N class engines and 300 25-ton trucks should have commenced.'

3. Harris, N.C. 'The Trend of Design of Railway Locomotives'; paper presented to Institution of Engineers Conference, Melbourne, March 1931.

4. Proposal for 'Pocono' 4-8-4 type locomotive. R.S. Engineer's Office, Melbourne, 19 November 1935.

5. 'New H Class 4-8-4 Type Launched.' ARHS Bn 41, March 1941. 'New 4-8-4 in Regular Service – makes First Passenger Run,' ARHS Bn 43, May 1941.

6. Abbott, R.L. 'Steam Locomotive Performance,' ARHS Bn 307, May 1963 listed H class drawbar h.p. figures obtained by dynamometer car tests as 2400 (20 mph), 2950 (30 mph), 3200 (40 mph), 3200 (50 mph), 3100 (60 mph).

7. Author's corres.

8. Buckland, J.L. 'Reflections on Some Aspects of Australian Steam Locomotion,' ARHS Bn 429, July 1973: 'The H class (inside cylinder) valve gear was, by contrast (with the Gresley gear of D57 and S classes) easy to set and maintain, nor had to be dismantled and reassembled to work on the centre valve or cylinder. Certainly it resulted in a very nearly perfect even "beat".'

9. Andrew Ahlston entered Newport as apprentice fitter and turner in January 1908. In 1913 he was promoted Engineering assistant. On return from Army service in World War 1, he was appointed Engineer of Tests. In 1928 he became Assistant CME to Mr N.C. Harris, and in 1933 he was CME until his retirement in 1955.

10 Brown Coal Briquette Trials – Locomotive H220. Memorandum and Standing Test Reports, NML., CME's Office, R.S. 48/11835, 13

October 1948. Also, Dynamometer Car Tests - Locomotive H220, week ending 7-5-49 and Proposed program of black, brown briquette and brown pulverised coal tests - H220

11. 'Testing 4-8-4 on Western Line Freight,' *Railways of Australia*, June 1949.

12. Buckland, J.L. 'A Proposed Beyer-Garratt Express Locomotive for Victoria,' ARHS Bn 423, January 1973. To operate the Ararat line, at the VR's request, Beyer, Peacock in November 1946 submitted outline drawings and specifications of a Garratt locomotive with 18-ton axle load and ability to haul a 500-ton *Overland* up 1-in-48 grade at 30 mph. Cylinders (4) were 19 x 28 in., coupled wheels 5ft 6in dia., boiler pressure 220 lbs, grate area 68.3 sq ft.

13. 'North East line tests,' ARHS Bn 120, October 1947.

14. George, R. H220 talk, ARHS (Vic.Div.) Newsletter January 1998.

15. Corres with the late Les Haining. May 1993. Les Haining began his railway career at age of 14 years and was employed as a lad labourer, spending five years in the New Boiler Shop at Newport where his father was Acting Leading Hand in charge of H220 boiler construction.

16. ARHS (Vic) records.

17. Holmes, Lloyd. 'Some Memories of H220,' *Newsrail* February 1991. Also personal corres.

18. George F. Brown commenced as apprentice fitter and turner Newport in 1923; in 1937 promoted to Plant Engineer and in 1943 to Supt. Loco. Maintenance. He visited U.S.A. in 1950 to negotiate introduction of VR's first mainline diesels. He became CME in 1955 and in 1958 Commissioner, then Chairman of Commissioners (the last to hold this title) in 1967 until retirement in 1973. He was patron of the Railway Museum, situated in 'George F.Brown Park' North Williamstown.

19. Corres. with L.Holmes.

20. McWhinney, R., Corres. January 1998 re H220 crewing. 'Les Haining was a terrific engineman, he had only one way to drive and that was hard, so you got used to this but we worked as a team, never was a hard word spoken.'

CHAPTER TWO

1. The author's *Kings of the Iron Horse* (see bibliography) will provide further information on the life of Fred Shea and locomotive developments during his career in the Victorian and South Australian Railways. Extracts on Shea's carreer are taken from the book.

2. Though sometimes referred to as the 'Big Mikado', this was, obviously, incorrect as the 720 had the American Berkshire wheel arrangement. 'Mikado' became an unpatriotic term at World War 2 and the word 'MacArthur' replaced it.

3. Without booster, tractive effort stood at 43,000 lbs. Two specifications are quoted for the 720 grate area - 59 sq ft as originally built and, when fitted with a brick wall to reduce firebox space, 46.8 sq ft. It was estimated that the large grate area would be needed for the burning of Leigh Creek coal. SAR Plans and Drawings, Islington Workshops, 1927-82. National Archives, Adelaide. File D5231.

4. New 520 Class Locomotive. AHRS Bn 77, March 1944.

5. No 734 was involved in a spectacular head-on collision with Mikado 709 at Snowtown on 7 April 1945. In 1949 the Cyclone front end fitted to 734 added to the loco.'s massive appearance. When written off on 26 March 1958, the second lowest mileage of the class was recorded against 734 – a total of 411,094 miles (657,752km).

6. The Hills section of the South line presented eastbound traffic with a 1-in-45 grade and 10-chain curves equivalent to 1-in-37 over the 14 miles from Mitcham to Mt Lofty. Westbound traffic faced the grade on the 10 miles between Callington and Nairne.

7. Author's interview and corres.

8. The *SAR Officers' Magazine* of October, 1927 noted – 'The comparative statement of coal costs shows that this State is called upon to pay 22/8 per ton more for coal used by the Railways than any other Railways in the Commonwealth. Last year we used 267,666 tons of coal at a total cost of £565,544 which worked out at 42/3 per ton, as against 19/3 per ton in 1914. The report further indicates that had the Commissioner been able to purchase coal at the same average price as other Railways in the Commonwealth, a saving of £234, 303 would have been made.'

9. Author's interviews and corres.

10 Dieselisation began with the assembly of 19 English Electric locomotives at Islington Workshops in 1951, utilising

equipment imported from the U.K. Project cost was given as £800,000, of which £300,000 would be spent at Islington.

11. No 720, condemned on 9 June 1959 had recorded the class's top running mileage of 729,376 (1,167,000 km).

CHAPTER THREE

1. From Linked, *A Song of the Ribbons of Rail* by 'Dryblower,' published in *The Golden West*, December 1917.

2. Drivers found to be 'doping' locomotives water with caster oil were liable to sacking. To reduce the risk of priming, some enginemen carried small bottles of the banned substance in their waistcoat pockets and swigged mouthfuls into the tender tank, or injected it with a hypodermic syringe into the engine hosebag. Later a modified 'doping solution' was officially introduced. Author's interviews and corres.

3. Following Deane's early efforts, the CR's next reference to diesel power occurred in the Commissioner's 1924 report followed in 1945 by Commissioner Gahan that tenders would be called for 2 or 4 1000 hp diesel-electric locomotives. Following granting of a General Motors' licence and availability of dollar currency, construction of the 11 GM class began at Clyde's plant early in 1951. The first locomotive was completed in 108 working days, on 24 August 1951.

4. The author's *Road Through the Wilderness* (see bibliography) will supply further information on the early locomotives of the Trans-Australian Railway, while his *Man of Steam* and *Making the Railways* refer to the development of the C36 class.

5. Norris Bell, a Scot, had been Chief Civil Engineer of the Queensland Railways until his appointment, as Henry Deane's successor, to Engineer-in-Chief of Transcontinental construction 1914-17. Subsequently he was first Commissioner of the Commonwealth Railways 1917-29.

6. Adam, E., Water Problems with Steam Locomotives on Commonwealth Railways, ARHS Bulletin, June 1986.

7. The fast Trans-Australian Express service began on 4 June 1938.

8. Building of the C36 class is referred to in the author's biography of E.E. Lucy, *Man of Steam*.

9. Corres. with P.J. Hannaberry (1982) and F.J. Shea records consulted by the author.

10. In July-August, 1949 oil burning conversions were made to C classes 63, 65, 67, 68, 69.

11. Keith Smith, OBE, began a 50-year railway career as an apprentice fitter and turner in the Eveleigh Workshops, Sydney. After graduating with honours in mechanical engineering from Sydney University, his career as a locomotive engineer led him from NSW to Tasmania, and then in 1950 to appointment as CME of the Commonwealth Railways at Port Augusta. In 1960 he became Commissioner and in 1975 chairman of the newly formed Australian National Railways Commission until retirement in 1981.

12. Eric Adam, whose railway career began as an apprentice at Eveleigh Workshops moved from NSW to the Commonwealth Railways, Port Augusta in 1940. His appointments were Chief Draftsman, Works Manager, Loco. Supt., and CME in 1945-50.

CHAPTER FOUR

1. Young, H. 'Garratt locomotive proposed by Messrs Beyer Peacock Company Ltd England for N.S.W. Railways,' Principal Designing Engineer memo to CME, Eveleigh, 4 April 1928.

2. Young, H. 'Express Locomotives for NSW Railways,' memo to Secretary for Railways, 23 November 1936.

3. Ibid.

4. Young, H. 'The C.38 Class 4-6-2 Type Locomotive,' Inst. of Engineers Journal, Vol. 16, reporting paper presented Sydney, 15 March, 1944.

5. Graham, I.B. 'Express Garratts to Albury,' *Australian Railway Enthusiast*, December 1982. The author's *Making the Railways* (see bibliography) will supply further information on the career of Harold Young and locomotive developments during his time as CME.

6. Dept. Railways, Annual Reports 1946-50.

7. Harold Young in evidence to the Western Australian ASG Royal Commission hearings in Sydney 1946.

8. Sheahan, W., Acting Transport Minister reported in *SMH* 29 April 1949.

9. 'The AD-60 Class Garratt Locomotive,' ARHS Bn 178, August 1952.

10. Prior to joining the NSWGR in 1912, Harold Young's railway

career began in 1899 as an engineering cadet in the Locomotive, Car and Wagon Dept of the Great North of Scotland Railway Co. In 1905 he joined The Yorkshire Engineering Co., Sheffield as locomotive draftsman; then in 1906, personal assistant to general manager of Messrs Kerr Stuart and Co. of Stoke-on-Trent, specialising in workshop improvements. In 1909 he returned to his native Scotland as locomotive draftsman with the North British Locomotive Co., Glasgow.

11.   ARHS Resource Centre

12. 'NSW Garratts to be Nation's Most Powerful Locos.' Railways In Australia, June 1949.

13. ARHS (NSW) Resource Centre.

14. Ibid.

15. Ibid.

16. Ibid.

17. Ibid. W. Armstrong was the next CME.

18. Ibid.

19. Principal Modifications to the AD60 included increased coal capacity (14 to 18 tons), sound intensifiers (to detect noise of exploding detonators), additional loco. braking (fitted to inner bogie wheels), raised tractive effort (increasing coupled wheel axle load to 18 tons and cylinder diameter to 19 7/8 in.), and dual controls (duplication of crew positions) to enable Garratts to be worked bunker-first on certain lines. Modified engines could take an 1100-ton load from Broadmeadow to Gosford and 1500 tons from Glenlee to Rozelle.

20. Author's interviews.

21. First AD-60 withdrawn was 6012 in June 1955. Last in normal revenue service was 6042 taking a coal train from Awaba to Broadmeadow on 26 February 1973.

CHAPTER FIVE

Information in this chapter is taken from the author's own records of employment at North Melbourne Locomotive Depot, and in recounting personal experiences.

CHAPTER SIX

1. The B13 (old 'F' class) first appeared in 1883 from British builders, Dubs and Kitson, a total of 112 locomotives. The 'QR look' dated from reboilering in the early 1900s.

2. Author's interviews and corres.

3. In 1923 the QR's route mileage exceeded 6000; in 1929 it was listed as 6340 and in 1933 reached 6500 (10,400 km). QR locomotive stock increased from 666 in 1920 to 787 by 1930; in 1950 the figure was 797.

4. Charles F. Pemberton, b. India 1859, VR draftsman 1886-1890, Loco. Foreman, Ipswich 1891, Dist. Loco. Supt., Rockhampton, 1892; Dist. Loco. Supt. Townsville, 1899-1909; Loco. Supt., Sthn. Div., 1910, CME 1911-1915; Dep. Cmsr. Rockhampton,1916-18; CME 1918-21 (resigned). Regarded as an innovator, the McKeen car and a petrol loco. were introduced during his CME term. He was dismissed but reinstated after five days in June 1899 for appealing to the Premier against W.H. Nisbet's appointment as CME.

5. *Sir Wm. MacGregor* (692) in 1920 hauled a 10-car train carrying the Prince of Wales from Wallangarra to Brisbane. In 1927 the Duke and Duchess of York travelled behind 699 over the same route.

6. Commissioner Davidson in 1918 directed an inquiry into the acquisition of Garratt or Mallet type locomotives; this was but one of a number of occasions when the QR considered equipping with an articulated locomotive; however severe drawgear limitations helped to rule out a decision.

7. Joseph Henry Rees began as an Ipswich Workshops apprentice 1892, then draftsman 1899-1910, Chief Draftsman and relieving Works Manager 1910-1919, finally Loco. Engr., Brisbane; d 1953.

8. John Edmund Robinson, b.1857, Draftsman in Loco. Engr.'s office, Brisbane, 1890; Chief Draftsman, Ipswich 1910; Works Mgr. 1911-21, incl. Acting CME 1915-18 during Pemberton's absence; Works Mgr. 1921-25 (when 'CME' title dropped); ret. July 1925. QR loco. stock reached 714 during Robinsons's term of service.

9. In 1921 the QR's freight traffic reached 5.1 million tons.

10. Extension of the North Coast line through to Mackay helped to promote the second order for 19 locomotives. By 1924 the 1043-mile North Coast route was open from Brisbane to Cairns, making it at the time Australia's second longest unbroken mainline.

11. Apart from the difficulty of dealing with the long firebox, the C19's short cab was regarded as particularly uncomfortable. Other complaints judged the loco. to be rough riding and noisy (!). Though the short travel valves were not modified, an increase in piston valve diameter from 8 to $9^1/_2$ inches in 1935 improved steaming efficiency. 'Hungry boards' later raised tender coal capacity from 7 to 11 tons.

12. The C19 was authorised to work the Townsville Mail through to Rockhampton and with track improvements later through to Mackay. Working on the Western line to Roma began after track improvements in 1928.

13. First $B18^1/_4$ no.84 made a successful trial on the Sydney Mail from Brisbane to Toowoomba on 28 July, 1926.

14. The C19 and CC19 were combined to make a class of 29 locomotives. Conversions of C18 to CC19 were - 692 May, 1934; 693 April, 1937; 694 April 1942.

15. In 1955-56, eight C19 class were withdrawn.

16. Author's corres.

CHAPTER SEVEN

1. J.A. Ellis, the WAGR Commissioner, was appointed Director of Locomotive and Rolling Stock Construction for the Ministry of Munitions and member of the Commonwealth Land Transport Board. Ellis had Mills, his CME, seconded to CLTB to undertake the design of the new Standard Garratt.

2. *Australian Standard Garratt Locomotives*, Report by the Royal Commissioner, Mr Justice A.A. Wolff. West Australian Votes and Proceedings, report No.11, 1946. Evidence presented to the Commission indicated that some 84% of WAGR motive power had reached or exceeded the 30-year economic life of a steam locomotive.

3 - 7 Ibid

8. 'The ASG Locomotive,' ARHS BN 71, September 1943. Also Minchin, R.S. 'Some Aspects of the Australian Standard Garratt Locomotive,' ARHS Bn 498, April 1979.

9. Wolff, J. Royal Commission report.

10. Author's corres. and F.J. Shea records.

11. QR wartime traffic had peaked in 1942-43. Annual Report showed earnings of £17,148,196 with a surplus of £4,566,151. Loco. mileage was 24,309,794 (v. 16,081,602 in 1939-40.) Average daily loaded wagon mileage was 53 (v. 29 in 1939-40).

12. Op. cit. Wolff, J .

13. Ibid.

14. Evidence to W.A. Royal Commission into ASG Locomotives, Sydney hearings 1946.

15. Author's corres. with Emu Bay Co. and Aust. Cement Ltd.

16. 'S Class Mixed Traffic 4-8-2 Locomotives.' ARHS Bn 83, September 1944. J.W.R. Broadfoot was CME when the design of the S class commenced. He was CME 1929-39. He was previously Works Manager, Midland, from 1920.

17. 'World Wide Engineering Competition,' *Railway and Tramway Magazine*, Perth, 1 December, 1938.

18. Mills, F. 'Some Factors Affecting Locomotive Design in Western Australia,' *Journal of the Institution of Locomotive Engineers*, Vol XXVII, No 135, Jan-Feb 1937. Detailed outline and specifications of a 4-8-2 indicated the advancement towards a detailed S class design. The WAGR Annual Report also referred to progress in the scheme to replace obsolete rolling stock.

19. 541 Bruce, 542 Bakewell, 543 Brockman, 544 Hallowell, 545 Dale, 546 Egerton, 547 Lindsay, 548 Gardner, 549 Greenmount, 550 Hardie.

20. Though S class coupled wheelbase totalled 13ft 6in, elimination of flanges on the first and third pairs reduced rigid wheelbase to nine ft. Yet in another calculation, Mills indicated a 15ft 10in rigid wheelbase could be accommodated with four coupled flanged wheels on a 5-chain curve.

21. WAGR's 1940 Annual Report forecast completion of the first S class in October 1941, with production following at one a month. However defence requirements (particularly involving a shortage of steel castings and blooms) delayed the schedule until 1943 when the first three engines were delivered.

22. The *West Australian*, 24 January and 1 March, 1948; Enginemen's union instanced unserviceability, excessive time under repair and derailments. The narrow single track confines of the Swan View tunnel caused problems for many crews, especially on the large dimensioned S class. Retired driver Harold Tower, while firing a new S for Driver Tom Priestman in February, 1943 recalled that their train was a test run with maximum allowable freight load. They were held at Swan View to allow a smaller train to come down the hill, which prevented the usual practice of 'making a dash' at the tunnel. Inside the tunnel, said Mr Tower, both were overcome by fumes, suffered burns to the back of their necks, noses,

throats, lungs and eyes and needed first aid in the brake van once the train cleared the tunnel.

23. Author's discussions and corres. with late R.S. Minchin 1982-84.

CHAPTER EIGHT

1. Herbert William Garratt was born in London on June 8, 1864. He served an apprenticeship from 1879-82 in the locomotive works of the North London Railway. Over the next 25 years his career took him to sea as a ship's engineer and included eight years with South American railways and a term as Loco. Superintendent of the Cuban Central Railways. His appointment on 7 August 1907 as Inspecting Engineer for the New South Wales Government Railways brought him into contact with Beyer, Peacock and Company. His patent for an articulated locomotive was deposited at the patent office on 24 January 1908. His agreement with Beyer, Peacock was signed on 18 September 1908. See also 'Compound Engines in Australia and New Zealand,' Part VII, ARHS Bn 67, May 1943

2. Most powerful locomotives on the 3ft 6in (1067mm) gauge in Australia in the 1920s were BHP's imported two Mikado (2-8-2) type, weighing 145 tons and exerting 37,845 lbs tractive effort. Baldwin of Philadelphia built four of the locos for the 35-mile Iron Knob mineral tramway from Whyalla to Iron Knob, S.A.

3. Buckland, J. 'Industrial Locomotives Built by Perry Engineering Co., Adelaide,' ARHS Bn June 1986.

4. The R class were withdrawn and scrapped 1951-57. None is preserved.

5. *Australian Standard Garratt Locomotives*. Report by the Royal Commissioner, Mr Justice Wolff. Parliament of Western Australia, Votes and Proceedings, report no 11, 1946.

6. Ibid. Mr Justice Wolff: 'When giving evidence Mr Mills, the (ASG) designer stated that ... Tasmania had agreed that certain locomotives that were being built to its order with the Clyde Engineering Company of Sydney should be set aside. Mr Mills could not have known the true facts when he made this statement. It is quite clear from records, which I saw, that the Tasmanian Government was compelled to accept the position. It will thus be seen how little there was of agreement on the part of the Tasmanian Government.'

7. The Q class were scrapped between 1962-68 except for Q5, sold to the Tasmanian Transport Museum, Glenorchy in 1968. At withdrawal in 1962, its mileage totalled 955,876 (1,529,400 km).

CHAPTER NINE

1. Graham, I.B., 'Express Garratts to Albury', Australian Railway Enthusiast Magazine, December 1982. Beyer-Garratt Articulated Locomotives, Manchester Beyer Peacock, 1947.

2. Cardew, C.A., 'The Progressive Development of the Steam Locomotive (and its Equipment) on the New South Wales Railways', Paper delivered to Northern Sub-Branch of Inst. Mech. Engrs., 19.1.1965. Also Thompson J.B., '38' The C38 Pacific Locomotives of the NSWGR, Sydney, Eveleigh Press, 1992.

3. Young, Harold, 'High Speed Railway Transport, including a Description of the Diesel Train of the New South Wales Railways', paper delivered to the Sydney Division, Inst. Engrs., October 1937.

4. 'The C.38 Class 4-6-2 Type Locomotive', paper given at Inst. Engrs, Sydney meeting, 15 March, 1944.

5. C.C. Lucy papers, author's research collection.

6. *A Compendium of NSW Steam Locomotives* (compiled by A. Grunbach) ARHS (NSW Div.), 1989.

7. ARHS Bulletin No. 442, 'Hand-fired Steam Loco Performance' (R.L. Abbott), August 1974. Also, '38 Class Working on the Melbourne Expresses' (by a Contributor), RTM, Roundhouse, July 1993.

8. Author's interview and corres, with D. Thurlow.

9. Sun-Herald, 26.7.1970. The original news item said 'Mr. R.T. Russell of Neutral Bay, now aged 80, assisted by Mr. R. Richardson and a 10-man team produced the design of the C38 (and) ... they obtained the idea of the bullet nose from France'.

10. Other post-war Pacifics on the narrow gauge were the Pm/Pmr of Western Australia (1950) and the M class of Tasmania (1952) – both imported from the U.K.

11. Data from QR Historical Centre, Ipswich and author's research files.

CHAPTER TEN

1. Author's collection. F.J. Shea papers.

2. Ibid.

3. Author's corres. With C. Huggan and late J.L. Buckland.

4. ANR staff magazine April 1955.

5. Port Dock Station Railway Museum Archives, 520 data.

6. Ibid.

7. *Advertiser* files, Mortlock Library, Adelaide.

8. Author's corres and discussion with W Holmesby. Raymond Loewy, a leading American Industrial designer was engaged by the PRR in 1936 to improve the exterior styling of its locomotives.

9. Port Dock Station Railway Museum Archives.

10. Ibid.

11. W. Holmesby.

12. *Advertiser* files, Mitchell Library, Sydney.

13. Reported in *The Locomotive Journal* of the AFULE, 8 October 1970.

BIBLIOGRAPHY

Armstrong, J. Locomotives in the Tropics, Brisbane, ARHS (Qld.) 1994.

Bermingham, P. The ML2 Story, Melbourne, Railway Traction Research Group, 1982.

Beyer-Garratt Articulated Locomotives, Manchester, Beyer, Peacock, 1947.

Burke, D. The Observer's Book of Steam Locomotives of Australia, London and New York, Frederick Warne, 1979.

Burke, D. Kings of the Iron Horse, Sydney, Methuen Australia 1985.

Burke, D. Road Through the Wilderness, Sydney, NSW University Press, 1991.

Burke, D. Making the Railways, Sydney, State Library of NSW Press, 1995.

Daddow, V. The Puffing Pioneers, Brisbane, University of Queensland Press, 1975.

Carlisle, R. and Abbott, R. Hudson Power, Melbourne, ARHS (Vic.) 1985.

Fluck, R. et al. Locomotives and Railcars of the Commonwealth Railways, Adelaide, Port Dock Station Railway Museum, 1996.

Groves, K., Wright, H., Morahan, M., The 60 Class, Sydney, NSW Rail Transport Museum, 1994.

Grunbach, A. (compiler). A Compendium of NSW Steam Locomotives, Sydney, ARHS (N.S.W.), 1989.

Gunzburg, A. A History of WAGR Steam Locomotives, Perth, ARHS (W.A.), 1984.

Harrigan, L. Victorian Railways to '62, Melbourne, Victorian Railways, 1962.

Kerr, J. Triumph of Narrow Gauge, Brisbane, Boolarong Publications, 1990.

Murray, J. Phoenix to the World, Sydney, Playright Publications, 1992.

McKillop, R. (compiler). Heritage Railways and Museums, Sydney, ARHS (N.S.W.), 1997.

Oberg, L. Locomotives of Australia, Sydney, Kangaroo Press, 1996.

Rae, L. A History of Railways and Tramways on Tasmania's West Coast, L. Rae, 1983.

Turton, K. Six and a Half Inches from Destiny, Melbourne, ARHS Vic.) 1973.

West, A. Crimson Giants, Brisbane, ARHS (Qld.), 1995.

OTHER REFERENCES

The monthly Bulletin of the Australian Railway Historical Society (ARHS). Annual Reports of Commonwealth and State railways, 1930-1955. Misc newspapers, including *Sydney Morning Herald* (SMH).

Burtrims, R. Australia's Garratt, Melbourne, Geelong Steam Preservation Society and ARHS (Vic.) 1975.

Colquhoun, D., Stewien, R., Thomas, A. 700 (Locomotive Series), Adelaide, ARHS (S.A.), 1979.

Cooper, G., Goss, G. Tasmanian Railways 1871-1996, Launceston, CG Publishing, 1996.

Commonwealth Railways, Adelaide, Mile End Railway Museum, 1972.

Gunzburg, A., WAGR Locomotives, 1940-68, Perth, ARHS (W.A.) 1968.

West, A. Made in Maryborough, Ipswich, ARHS (Qld.), 1994.

Western Australian Preserved Locomotives, Adelaide, Railmac Publications, 1983.

THE AUSTRALIAN RAILWAY HISTORICAL SOCIETY
New South Wales Division

About the Society

The Australian Railway Historical Society, New South Wales Division, had its beginnings in 1933 with the formation of the Railway Circle of Australasia. Since then it has grown to become one of the largest railway societies in the country. Autonomous Divisions exist in each State and the Australian Capital Territory, and there is a branch of the NSW Division in Newcastle. The Society's main objectives are: to promote the association of persons interested in the history and operations of railways for their mutual benefit and enjoyment; to encourage the study of Australian railways and the compilation and maintenance of authentic records; to maintain an archives collection, to produce books, periodicals, etc., of railway interest (including the ARHS *Bulletin* and *Railway Digest*) and to arrange rail tours and excursions.

Meetings of members and their guests are held monthly in Sydney and Newcastle and in the other capitals. These meetings usually feature a talk on a topic of railway interest, often accompanied by a programme of films or slides.

The ARHS Resource Centre of the NSW Division, housing thousands of documents, photographs, periodicals and books, and the Bookshop are at 67 Renwick Street, Redfern, 2016.

Other Divisions of the Australian Railway Historical Society

Australian Capital Territory	Box 112, PO Civic Square, ACT 2608
Victoria	GPO Box 5177AA, Melbourne, Vic. 3001
Queensland	Box 682, GPO Brisbane, Qld. 4001
South Australia	Box 507, GPO Adelaide, SA 5001
Western Australia	PO Box 363, Bassendean, WA 6054
Tasmania	PO Box 162, Sandy Bay, Tas. 7005

BY THE SAME AUTHOR

Monday at McMurdo
Come Midnight Monday
Darknight
Railways of Australia
Great Steam Trains of Australia
Full Steam Across the Mountains
Changing Trains
The Observer's Book of Steam Locomotives
Man of Steam
Kings of the Iron Horse
With Iron Rails
Road Through the Wilderness
The World of Betsey Throsby
Making the Railways
Moments of Terror: The Story of Antarctic Aviation
Juggernaut!
Dreaming of the Resurrection: A Reconciliation Story
Life of Mary Ward (video)
Great Scott! (musical)
Julian: A Man Condemned? (dramatisation)

INDEX